TEMPLE RUN

Race Through Time to Unlock Secrets of Ancient Worlds

TRACEY WEST

SELECT ILLUSTRATIONS
BY GONZALO ORDÓÑEZ

AN OFFICIAL
KIDS' COMPANION
TO THE GAME
TEMPLE RUN

NATIONAL GEOGRAPHIC
Washington, D.C.

CONTENTS

 # EXPLORE THE ANCIENT WORLD WITH TEMPLE RUN!

The fictional world of the Temple Run game meets the real world in this book! National Geographic Kids and Temple Run have teamed up to bring you real-life facts and information about how the ancients lived. So, while you read about adventures with Guy Dangerous and Scarlett Fox, check out how people really lived back then and learn about their world. Just watch out for those demon monkeys!

>>> MEET YOUR GUIDES >>>

GUY DANGEROUS

Adventure seems to follow Guy wherever he goes! But he's a good-hearted hero whose curiosity often leads him into danger. Fortunately, his strong will and resourcefulness help him see another day. Meet Guy in Angkor and at Göbekli Tepe.

SCARLETT FOX

Scarlett is a natural-born leader determined to win at any cost. Cunning and organized, she uses her sharp wits to achieve her goals. Meet Scarlett at Stonehenge and in Egypt.

BARRY BONES

Justice has a good friend in Barry, a street-smart cop who's seen it all—until now. He works tirelessly to fight for what's right. Meet Barry in Greece, China, and Petra.

KARMA LEE

Karma is a royal leader, since she's an heiress of the greatest dynasty of the 22nd century. But she's also a scholar trained in world culture and martial arts who uses her skills to help others. Meet Karma in Rome and at Chichén Itzá.

MARIA SELVA

Spunky and smart Maria is always exploring the outdoors and snapping as many photos as she can. She always carries at least two cameras and her smartphone so she's got everything covered from all angles. Meet Maria in Machu Picchu and Tenochtitlan.

A MYSTERIOUS IDOL

ANGKOR, CAMBODIA: PRESENT DAY

"Found it!" you yell, your voice bouncing off the walls of the old stone temple. You've been exploring the ruins of the ancient city of Angkor, Cambodia, for months now, since a tip came in that there was something special hidden away here. Now you hold the item in your hands.

You unwrap the dusty fabric covering it and reveal an idol. It's a skull carved out of pure gold, with big, bulging eyes, and an open mouth showing lots of teeth.

"Aaaaaiiiiiieeeeeeeeee!"

You quickly turn around as the strange, unearthly howl echoes through the temple. And then you see them.

They look like monkeys. Or demons. Or demon monkeys, maybe, with black, matted fur, huge glowing eyes, and long fangs. And they're charging at you!

You race out of the temple onto a stone walkway, as fast as your legs can carry you.

The path cuts sharply to the right and you make the turn, confusing the demon monkeys for a few seconds. You spot an opening in a crumbling building and run inside.

The door slams and you see a tall man with red hair and blue eyes.

"Guy Dangerous! Is that really you?" you ask. You'd recognize that famous explorer anywhere.

"No time for introductions," he says in a gruff voice. "You woke up those monkeys. Not just here, but in temples all over the world—threatening everyone! Now you've got to fix it."

He takes the idol from you and turns it so you can see the back of the head. There are ten round indentations.

"You can use the idol to stop the demon monkeys, but it's got to be complete," he tells you. "You need to travel through time to find the ten missing gems."

Your mind is spinning. "Travel through time? How?"

Guy presses on the idol's head. A bright light spills out of the skull's open mouth.

"It's a time portal," he says, pointing to one of the empty circles on the back of the idol's head. "Look."

A symbol appears in the circle. It looks like a cave drawing of a wild boar.

"The symbol will tell you where to go," he says. Then he takes the watch off of his wrist and hands it to you. "And this will tell you where you are. And where to look. Kind of like a homing beacon."

"But . . but . . . " you stammer.

"No buts," he says. "Or the demon monkeys rule the world. Got it?"

You nod.

"Don't worry, I'll help you get started," Guy tells you.

"Aaaaaiiiiiieeeeeeeeee!"

Guy presses the button on the idol and hands it to you. "I'll distract them. You go find us a safe place to reactivate the portal. Now run!"

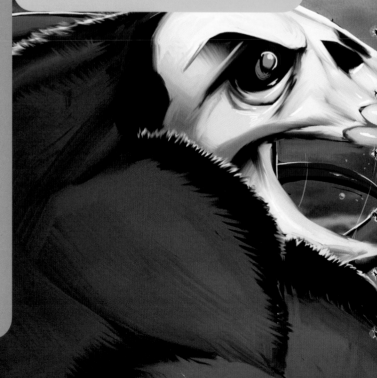

ANGKOR

YOUR **HEAD IS SPINNING** AS YOU RACE OUT OF THE CAVE. YOU TUCK THE IDOL INTO YOUR BACKPACK AS YOU **RACE FOR YOUR LIFE.**

The eerie wail of the demon monkeys echoes behind you, and you know they're on your trail. You and Guy Dangerous need to find a safe place to open the portal—but where? Even though you've been exploring the Angkor archaeological site for months, you've barely scratched the surface. It's a 386-square-mile (1,000-sq-km) complex of more than 60 temples in the ancient city of Angkor. It's easy to get lost among the crumbling stone ruins, dirt paths, stone walkways, and statues.

But maybe that's exactly what you need to do!

CAMBODIA

Angkor

MEKONG RIVER

TONLE SAP

CAMBODIA

Phnom Penh

GULF OF THAILAND

SOUTH CHINA SEA

0   100   200 miles
0   100   200 kilometers

Asia

CAMBODIA

LAOS

THAILAND

VIETNAM

MEKONG RIVER

CAMBODIA

GULF OF THAILAND

SOUTH CHINA SEA

Khmer Empire
Champa Kingdom

A MONUMENT TO RELIGION

Your heart feels as if it's pounding out of your chest as you try to outrace the demon monkeys. Then Guy appears from up ahead and points, "Get ready to ride!" You look on the side of the road—it's a remorque motorbike—a small motorcycle with a trailer attached to carry tourists. You hop in the driver's seat, and it starts right up. With the demon monkeys at your heels, you and Guy zoom toward the largest temple in Angkor—Angkor Wat. Your mind races as you struggle to remember what you know about it.

The entire Angkor-Wat complex covers more than 500 acres (202 ha).

A SACRED MOUNTAIN

The Khmer Empire thrived in southeast Asia from the 9th to the 15th centuries A.D. The empire was based in what we know today as Cambodia. Shortly after Khmer King Suryavarman II was crowned in 1113, he ordered workers to begin construction on the Angkor Wat temple. It was built to honor the Hindu god Vishnu and to become the king's tomb after he died.

The tallest tower in the center symbolizes Mount Meru, the mountain that Hindus believe is at the center of the universe and home of the gods. The four smaller towers around it represent the mountain's other peaks.

To get to the towers, you'd have to get past a moat and two stone-wall enclosures. The outer wall, also called the gallery, is carved with scenes from Vishnu's life, symbols and stories of the Hindu religion, and scenes from Suryavarman's battles.

WHO WAS SURYAVARMAN II?

During his reign, this king of the Khmer Empire led his army into many battles to expand the rule of what is now Cambodia. He extended his reign into parts of what is now Thailand. He took over the kingdom of Champa in 1145, but the Chams allied with the Vietnamese and fought back. (The Champa kingdom went on to become part of Vietnam.) Suryavarman battled the Chams until his death in 1150, and it is believed his remains may have been buried in the Angkor Wat temple.

Most of the other temples in Angkor were swallowed up by the jungle over the centuries.

VISHNU THE PROTECTOR

There are many gods in the Hindu religion, but three gods are said to have a special role in controlling the universe: Brahma the Creator, Vishnu the Protector, and Shiva the Destroyer. When things get out of balance on Earth, it's said Vishnu will appear to help fight evil. He sometimes takes a human form. In his godly form, he often appears with blue skin and four arms. He is married to Lakshmi, goddess of wealth, fortune, and purity.

Vishnu is often pictured lying on or sitting underneath a multiheaded snake. He looks happy and peaceful, symbolizing the ability to stay calm in the face of danger.

DEADLY SNAKES

>>> The engine of the remorque hums as you zip around the outer wall of the Angkor Wat temple, searching for the west gate. "I think we've lost the demon monkeys," Guy says, relieved. But when you turn the corner, a bunch of them are charging right toward you!

Startled, you try to turn around, and the bike skids underneath you. You've lost control. The bike goes spinning off down the path, and you and Guy go rolling into Angkor Wat's moat.

Luckily, you both can swim. Exhausted, you crawl onto the grass on the other side. When you lift your head, you see the eyes of a snake staring at you! You scramble to your feet. Cambodia is home to several deadly snakes—and this could be one of them.

RUSSELL'S VIPER

HABITAT: Farmlands
SIZE: Up to 5 feet (1.5 m) long
DIET: Rodents and other small animals

Thousands of people each year die from the bite of this snake.

WHITE-LIPPED PIT VIPER

The bite from this snake isn't usually fatal—but it can be very painful. The snake lives in wooded and bushy areas near human settlements.

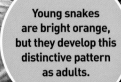

Young snakes are bright orange, but they develop this distinctive pattern as adults.

This cobra gets its name from the pattern on the back of its hood, which looks like an eye with an eyeglass lens surrounding it.

The venom of a monacled cobra causes the victim's organs and muscles to quickly break down, causing death to come swiftly.

MONACLED COBRA

HABITAT: Wet places such as swamps and paddy fields

SIZE: Up to 6.5 feet (2 m) long

DIET: Birds, small mammals, and other snakes

KING COBRA
Growing up to 18 feet (5.5 m) long, the king cobra is the world's largest venomous snake. It is active during the day and will attack if provoked.

BANDED KRAIT
This snake's venom is poisonous, but these shy creatures are nocturnal hunters and are not aggressive. They can be identified by alternating black bands and yellow bands, which are the same width.

TA PROHM TEMPLE

"Back away slowly," says Guy. Dripping wet, you quietly move away from the snake. It doesn't pursue you. Relieved, you lead the way toward the quietest place you know in Angkor: the temple of Ta Prohm. Over the ages, the jungle has been allowed to grow over the temple. Giant tree roots push apart walls and block doorways; branches cover the stone temple like a canopy. You lead Guy into a dark corridor and a thick blanket of quiet surrounds you both.

Scenes from the movie *Tomb Raider* were filmed in Ta Prohm.

ANGKOR'S BUDDHIST TEMPLES

Jayavarman VII ruled the Khmer Empire for nearly 40 years, from A.D. 1181–1220. A follower of the Buddhist religion, he improved the city of Angkor—building hospitals, roads, and more—and erected many Buddhist temples. Ta Prohm is a Buddhist temple that he built for his mother. Over the centuries, the jungle became intertwined with the temple, and many think that has only made it more beautiful.

TEMPLE STATS

BUILT: In the late 12th century A.D.

LOCATION: In Angkor, Cambodia, east of the Angkor Thom complex

WHO MADE IT: King Jayavarman VII

DEDICATED TO: The king's mother

TURKEY

BLACK SEA

Istanbul

Ankara

T U R K E Y

Konya
Çatalhöyük

Şanlıurfa

Göbekli Tepe

Europe   Asia

TURKEY

MEDITERRANEAN

SEA

0   100   200 miles

0   100   200 kilometers

MYSTERIOUS MONOLITHS

For a second, you're so freaked out that you almost forget why you're here. "Remember," says Guy, "get the gem and get out. We've got the world to save. I'll take watch." Without another word he heads toward the outskirts of the site.

You decide to start with the stone pillars. As you get closer, you see that they're carved with images of animals. "What is this place?" you wonder out loud.

You slowly walk the circular path around the monoliths. It's kind of creepy in the dark.

THESE ANIMAL SCULPTURES ARE CALLED BAS-RELIEFS, IN WHICH THE BACKGROUND IS FLAT AND THE CARVED OBJECT SEEMS TO PROJECT SLIGHTLY FROM THE BACKGROUND.

Göbekli Tepe means "belly hill" in Turkish.

The animals on the stones include gazelles, foxes, snakes, scorpions, ducks, lions, and wild boars.

GÖBEKLI TEPE
9000 B.C.

These stones are carved from limestone. Today, limestone is used to make cement.

THE HIGHEST T-SHAPED STONES ARE 18 FEET (5.5 M) HIGH AND SOME WEIGH 16 TONS (14.5 MT), ABOUT AS MUCH AS A SCHOOL BUS LOADED WITH ELEMENTARY SCHOOL STUDENTS.

TEMPLE STATS

BUILT: About 11,600 years ago

LOCATION: Turkey, near the border of Syria

PRONUNCIATION: Guh-behk-LEE TEH-peh

WHO MADE IT: People from hunter-gatherer tribes

PURPOSE: Many experts think this was one of the first religious sites ever built. Archaeologists are still excavating the area to uncover its mysteries.

WHAT IS GÖBEKLI TEPE?

Was Göbekli Tepe the first religious temple ever created by humans? Archaeologist Klaus Schmidt thinks so. He has studied Göbekli Tepe since the 1990s. He cites several reasons for this theory, including the T-shaped pillars, which he says represent humans. They are in a circle, the way that humans would have stood in a circle at a religious meeting or dance. If he is right, this makes Göbekli Tepe one of the most important ancient sites in the world.

Whatever the site was used for, the effort involved in its construction is evidence that the site must have been very important to the people who built it. They were most likely nomads who survived by gathering wild plants and hunting. So how did they cut the T shapes into the stone? And how did they carve the animals? Primitive stone and flint tools were found at the site, but scientists aren't exactly sure. How did the people lug the stones to the site on top of the hill? They didn't have wheels or domesticated animals like donkeys to haul things. Much of this important site is still a mystery!

21

< EXPLORE >
ÇATALHÖYÜK

While Göbekli Tepe might be the world's first religious site, north of this monument is a site that is likely one of the world's first cities: Çatalhöyük.

Archaeologists believe that people of the Neolithic period started building the mud-brick homes in Çatalhöyük about 9,000 years ago. A British archaeologist named James Mellaart excavated the site in the 1960s. Inside the homes, he found platforms for sleeping and ovens for cooking. It is believed that 6,000 people could have lived at the site.

In addition to the homes, murals, sculptures, and other artifacts have been found at Çatalhöyük.

Imagine a city with no roads! Excavations at Çatalhöyük show that the city was streetless and people actually entered the closely packed, mud-brick buildings from the roof.

FIND THIS NEOLITHIC DAGGER IN THE TEMPLE RUN GAME!

ANCIENT TREASURES

NEOLITHIC FINDS

FIGURES: Figures have been found showing women holding animals. This one is seated on a throne flanked by lions or other big cats.

DAGGERS: Daggers like this one were made of flint, a hard, gray rock. The shape was slowly chipped away with another stone, much like a whittler's technique of carving a shape out of wood with a knife.

MURALS: Archaeologists found murals painted on the walls of buildings. Before then, people painted on cave walls. These are the first "house paintings" ever discovered, and could be the oldest in the world.

Early Neolithic people also made things out of animal bones: tools, such as needles for sewing and weaving, as well as ornaments that could be worn like jewelry.

OBSIDIAN TOOLS

A tool like this one would have been used to scrape the hair or flesh from animal hides. The tools were often made of obsidian, a volcanic glass that can be as sharp as a razor. Some stone scrapers had a wooden handle attached.

THE STONE AGE

>>> You notice a bright red light blinking on the face of the watch Guy gave you. What had he said? A homing beacon. Right. You test it out. When you walk in one direction, the light starts to dim. But when you change direction, it gets brighter. The gem must be near . . .

Suddenly you spot something glittering in one of the monoliths. It's a perfectly round, black gem, embedded in the stone above a carving of a wild boar. Could this be it?

The first cave paintings come from the Paleolithic period. For "paint," ancient artists ground up yellow and red pigments they found in rocks, and mixed the powder with their spit.

WELCOME TO THE STONE AGE

When archaeologists talk about the Stone Age, they're referring to the period of human history when people figured out how to make tools out of stone. Archaeologists think that happened about two million years ago.

Most of the Stone Age takes place in the Paleolithic period, or the Old Stone Age. Then, about 12,000 years ago, the Neolithic, or New Stone Age began. People in both ages used stone tools, but there are some major differences in the way the people lived.

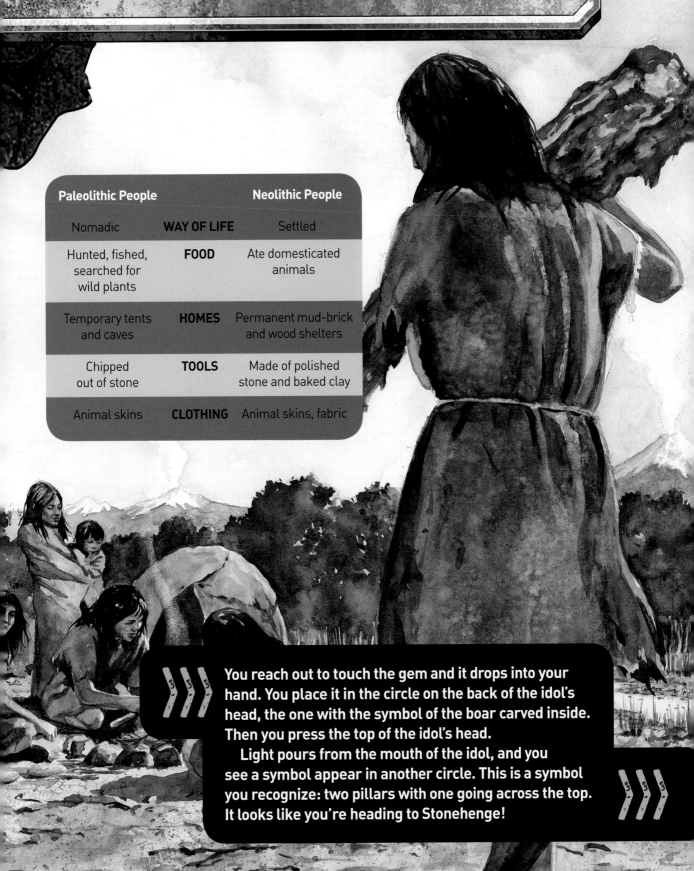

Paleolithic People		Neolithic People
Nomadic	WAY OF LIFE	Settled
Hunted, fished, searched for wild plants	FOOD	Ate domesticated animals
Temporary tents and caves	HOMES	Permanent mud-brick and wood shelters
Chipped out of stone	TOOLS	Made of polished stone and baked clay
Animal skins	CLOTHING	Animal skins, fabric

You reach out to touch the gem and it drops into your hand. You place it in the circle on the back of the idol's head, the one with the symbol of the boar carved inside. Then you press the top of the idol's head.

Light pours from the mouth of the idol, and you see a symbol appear in another circle. This is a symbol you recognize: two pillars with one going across the top. It looks like you're heading to Stonehenge!

1590 B.C.

THE IDOL **TRANSPORTS YOU,** AND AS THE LIGHT STARTS TO FADE AGAIN, YOU GLANCE AT YOUR WATCH.

>>> It's 1590 B.C. You've jumped ahead in time more than 7,000 years!

You look up, and the sun is shining. There's green grass between your feet, and you can see the tall pillars of Stonehenge up ahead. Guy is nowhere to be seen. But you see a figure walking toward you, and you tense. She's a tall woman with her red hair pulled back in a ponytail, and she's dressed in modern clothing.

"Hey kid," she says. "I was exploring Stonehenge and the next minute I'm here and instead of crumbling ruins, everything's brand new. You got something to do with it?

"I-I'm not sure," you stammer. "I used a time portal to get here. Guy Dangerous gave it to me. Where is he?"

The woman raises an eyebrow. "Name's Scarlett Fox. Maybe you'd better tell me the whole story."

UNITED KINGDOM — Europe

ATLANTIC OCEAN

SCOTLAND

NORTH SEA

NORTHERN IRELAND

UNITED KINGDOM

IRISH SEA

WALES

ENGLAND

Avebury

Stonehenge

London

RIVER AVON

CELTIC SEA

ENGLISH CHANNEL

STONEHENGE ACROSS TIME

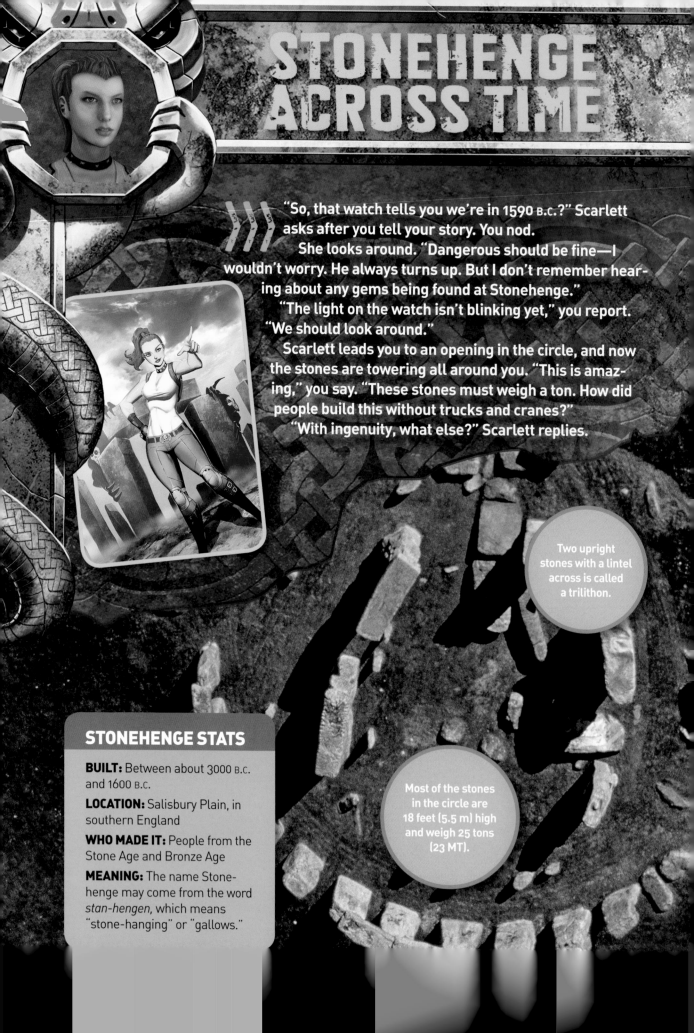

"So, that watch tells you we're in 1590 B.C.?" Scarlett asks after you tell your story. You nod.

She looks around. "Dangerous should be fine—I wouldn't worry. He always turns up. But I don't remember hearing about any gems being found at Stonehenge."

"The light on the watch isn't blinking yet," you report. "We should look around."

Scarlett leads you to an opening in the circle, and now the stones are towering all around you. "This is amazing," you say. "These stones must weigh a ton. How did people build this without trucks and cranes?"

"With ingenuity, what else?" Scarlett replies.

Two upright stones with a lintel across is called a trilithon.

Most of the stones in the circle are 18 feet (5.5 m) high and weigh 25 tons (23 MT).

STONEHENGE STATS

BUILT: Between about 3000 B.C. and 1600 B.C.

LOCATION: Salisbury Plain, in southern England

WHO MADE IT: People from the Stone Age and Bronze Age

MEANING: The name Stonehenge may come from the word *stan-hengen*, which means "stone-hanging" or "gallows."

CENTURIES IN THE MAKING

The creation of Stonehenge began sometime around 3000 B.C. by Neolithic people. Over the centuries, some stones were added, and others were taken down. People of the Bronze Age made the last changes sometime around 1600 B.C. Here's how the monument changed over time:

STEP ONE: THE HENGE (AROUND 3000 B.C.)

Salisbury Plain is a plateau in central southern England that covers about 300 square miles (777 sq km). The first builders of Stonehenge began by digging a circular ditch in the chalky earth to make a circle 375 feet (114 m) across, called a "henge." Then they built a raised bank inside the circle, right next to the ditch. Inside the bank are 56 circular holes called Aubrey Holes. They might have contained wood posts or stone pillars. Two openings in the circle were used as entrances.

STEP TWO: WOOD POSTS (AROUND 3000 B.C.)

Tall wood posts were arranged in patterns inside the circle. Archaeologists think that Stonehenge might have been used as a cemetery during this time. This also might be the time that the Heelstone was placed by the northeast entrance. It's a tall sarsen stone—a sandstone that is like cement. A sandstone known as the Altar Stone was probably placed around this time, too.

STEP THREE: BLUESTONES (AROUND 2500 B.C.)

Bluestones are named because they appear to be blue when they're wet. The bluestones were arranged in a circle in the middle of the larger circle.

STEP FOUR: THE SARSEN CIRCLE (AROUND 2500 B.C.)

This is when Stonehenge started to take the shape we know it as today. Two circles of sarsen stones replaced the bluestones. The first circle was made of 30 stones, each 16 feet (5 m) tall, and topped by stones called lintels. Inside that circle was a semicircle of five pairs of stones. Each pair was separate from the other, but connected by a lintel. The tallest of these stones was 25 feet (8 m) high. Also around this time, four sarsen stones known as the Station Stones were placed around the ring of Aubrey Holes.

STEP FIVE: A ROAD TO THE RIVER (AROUND 2400 B.C.)

During this period, a two-mile (3-km) path from the northeast entrance to the River Avon was created. It was dug in the same manner as the henge: ditches with banks along the side.

STEP SIX: REARRANGE THE BLUESTONES (AROUND 2200 B.C.)

Around this time, the bluestones that were removed before were arranged inside the first circle.

STEP SEVEN: MORE PITS (AROUND 2000 B.C.)

A ring of holes known as the Z holes was dug around the sarsen stone circle.

STEP EIGHT: EVEN MORE PITS (AROUND 1600 B.C.)

A second ring of holes, known as the Y holes, was dug around the Z holes.

PLORE >
BUILDING
STONEHENGE

endering shows what Stonehenge may
like during the solstice, with a shaft
t shining through the stones.

MYSTERY OF THE BLUESTONES

Scientists know the bluestones came from southwest Wales. But they can't agree on how they made the long journey to Salisbury Plain. Some speculate that humans dragged them across the land and then loaded them on rafts that traveled along the coast of Wales and then upriver—about a 160-mile (258-km) trek. But geologists think that glaciers might have pushed the stones from Wales to Salisbury long before humans inhabited the land.

ANCIENT TREASURES

THE KING OF STONEHENGE

In 2002, archaeologists made an amazing discovery about three miles (5 km) from Stonehenge, in a town called Amesbury. They found the grave of a man buried with many treasures: gold hair ornaments, copper knives, boars' tusks, pottery, and other tools. He was obviously a very important man. But who was he?

Scientists determined that he lived around 2300 B.C.—when Stonehenge was built. After testing his teeth, bones, and hair, they also discovered that he came from the Alps mountain range in the north. People dubbed him the "King of Stonehenge." Nobody is sure whether he played a role in Stonehenge. But the metal objects in his grave did tell archaeologists that the Bronze Age had reached England during the time of Stonehenge.

The scientific name for bluestone is spotted dolerite. It's an igneous rock—a rock that is formed when lava or magma hardens.

The surface of each pillar was pounded smooth with stone tools.

The heaviest bluestones weigh as much as four tons (3.6 MT).

THE SARSEN STONES

The sarsen stones were brought to Stonehenge from the Avebury area of England, which is about 25 miles (40 km) north. One theory is that the stones were transported by the use of leather ropes and a sledge—a platform on runners that gets pulled by work animals. In this case, it's believed that as many as 500 men may have been needed to pull one stone, plus another 100 men to move the rollers from back to front.

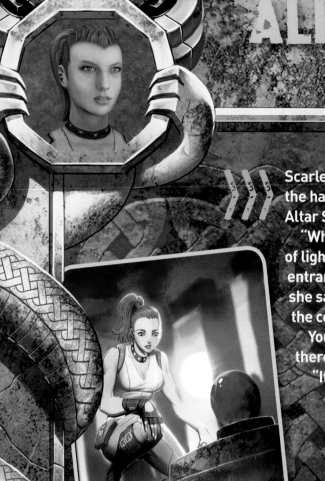

Scarlett walks over to the single, standing stone inside the half circle of trilithons: the stone known as the Altar Stone. Then she points.

"When the sun rises on the summer solstice, a shaft of light shines right between those two stones by the entrance—the Heel Stone and the Slaughter Stone," she says. "It shines right through the pillars and hits the center of the Altar Stone."

You walk over to the Altar Stone and look—and there, embedded in it, is a blue circle-shaped gem.

"It's the gem!" you cry.

> Today, more than one million visitors travel to Stonehenge each year.

THE SOLSTICES

In the Northern Hemisphere, the summer solstice is the day that the summer sun travels its longest path across the sky, making it the longest day of the year (usually June 20 or 21). The winter solstice is the day in the Northern Hemisphere when the sun travels its shortest path, making it the shortest day of the year (usually December 20 or 21).

Today, about 20,000 to 30,000 people each year visit Stonehenge on the summer solstice to watch the sun's rays hit the Altar Stone.

STONEHENGE 1590 B.C.

STONEHENGE THEORIES

Archaeologists have several theories about why Stonehenge may have been built.

A BURIAL SITE: The cremated remains of 60 people as well as 240 burials have been discovered at Stonehenge. It's clear that it was some kind of burial site. But was that all it was?

A HEALING SITE: Many of the people buried at Stonehenge suffered from diseases. Some scientists think they were brought to Stonehenge to be healed because bluestones were believed to have healing powers.

SOLAR CALENDAR: The stones are aligned to catch the sun's rays on the summer solstice and winter solstice.

TEMPLE OF THE DEAD: There is another large henge about two miles (3 km) from Stonehenge known as Durrington Walls. There are signs that great feasting took place at this site. One theory is that the two sites were linked: Durrington Walls represented life, and Stonehenge represented death.

Scarlett looks impressed as you take out the idol and put the gem in its place. When you activate the idol, a third symbol begins to glow in one of the circles. It's a ram's head.

Scarlett raises an eyebrow. "The ram was sacred to the Egyptians. Looks like we're going to Egypt."

EGYPT

1250 B.C.

YOUR STOMACH DROPS AS THE VORTEX SPITS YOU OUT INTO A PILE OF SOFT, HOT SAND.

Next to you, Scarlett lands on her feet. You stand up and gasp. A massive pyramid rising on the horizon catches your eye. "I guess we made it to Egypt," you say, looking at the watch Guy gave you. "It's 1250 B.C. But the watch isn't even blinking."

Scarlett looks thoughtful. "Egypt is a big place. But I'm betting we'll find the gem in one of the big temples here. They're all in Thebes, the capital city. That's about 400 miles [644 km] south."

Then you turn around and see the tallest building you've ever seen in your life.

MEDITERRANEAN SEA

LOWER EGYPT

Pyramids at Giza

EGYPT

MIDDLE EGYPT

Temple of
Amun-Re

Valley of the Kings

King Tut's tomb

Temple of
Luxor

UPPER EGYPT

NILE RIVER

RED SEA

EGYPT

Africa

0   100   200 miles
0   100   200 kilometers

THE PYRAMIDS OF GIZA

"Wow, I would really like to see what the inside of a pyramid looks like before we go," you say.

Scarlett Fox grins. "You think you have what it takes to break into one of those? These pyramids and other Egyptian tombs were designed with all kinds of blocks and traps for burglars."

"Yeah, but *you* could get us in," you say. "There's probably amazing stuff inside. Mummies. Treasure. Who knows what else?"

The Sphinx was buried up to its shoulders with sand until the 1930s, when an archaeologist finally dug it out.

KNOWN AS: Menkaure
BUILT FOR: Pharaoh Menkaure, circa 2490 B.C.
HEIGHT: 213 feet (65 m)

Of the seven wonders of the ancient world, the Great Pyramid is the only one left standing.

WHAT ARE THE PYRAMIDS?

These pyramids are great big tombs, built by Egyptian pharaohs to house their bodies and their most precious belongings. The Great Pyramid was the largest, most spectacular pyramid Egypt had ever seen. It took 20 years and at least 20,000 workers to build. Its white limestone outer walls—lost over time due to erosion and stripped by people for building materials—would have glittered against the blue sky.

The Great Pyramid is built from 2.3 million stone blocks each weighing an average of 2.5 to 15 tons (2.3 to 13.6 MT)!

KNOWN AS: Khafre
BUILT FOR: Pharaoh Khafre, circa 2520 B.C.
HEIGHT: 471 feet (144 m)

KNOWN AS: Great Pyramid, or Khufu
BUILT FOR: Pharaoh Khufu circa 2550 B.C.
HEIGHT: 481 feet (147 m)

THE SPHINX
GUARDIAN OF THE TOMBS

Khafre's pyramid might not have been as tall as his father Khufu's, but he made up for it with an impressive statue in front of it. The Great Sphinx has the body of a lion but the head of a man and headdress of a pharaoh. Workers carved the statue out of limestone and made the creature over 240 feet (73 m) long and 66 feet (20 m) high. Today, the sphinx is missing several of its original parts, including its nose and beard. But even without some of its face, the Great Sphinx still guards the tombs of the three ancient kings today.

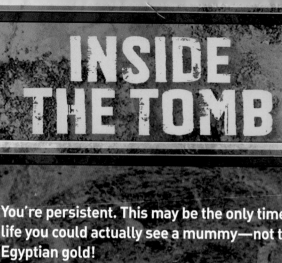

INSIDE THE TOMB

>>> You're persistent. This may be the only time in your life you could actually see a mummy—not to mention Egyptian gold!

Scarlett gets a gleam in her eye. "Okay, you've convinced me. But we can't stay long. We're on a mission, remember?"
She leads you through dark tunnels, twists and turns, up ladders, and over deadly booby-trapped pits. Scarlett stops suddenly at a bend and presses a hieroglyph. A secret door opens to a room filled with gold, gems, and a huge sarcophagus—the stuff of kings. Your mouth drops open.

"Welcome to the room of the dead," she smiles.

ANCIENT TREASURES

HEART AMULET

Priests might place an amulet—a small object believed to have magical powers—inside the bandages of a mummy. An amulet might have been intended to protect the spirit of the deceased or help them find happiness in the afterlife.

Heart-shaped amulets were placed with the mummy to protect its heart. It was believed that in the afterlife, the god Osiris could weigh the mummy's heart and determine if it belonged to a good or bad person.

Egyptians mummified hippopotamuses, apes, dogs, and cats, too!

HOW TO MAKE A MUMMY

Egyptians mummified their dead to preserve the body and prevent decay. According to Egyptian religion, the body housed a person's spirit; if the body were destroyed, that spirit could not enter the afterlife. Mummy makers were priests called embalmers, and would spend about 70 days creating a mummy, following these steps:

STEP 1. GOODBYE, ORGANS: Hook-shaped instruments were used to pull pieces of the brain out through the nostrils. The only organ left inside the body was the heart, because it was believed to contain the person's essence. The stomach, liver, lungs, and intestines were preserved in special containers called canopic jars.

STEP 2. DRY OUT BODY: Embalmers packed the organless body with a type of salt called natron. The salt soaked up all the body's moisture in about 40 days. The salt was then removed and the body stuffed with spices, rags, and plants.

STEP 3. WRAP, WRAP, WRAP: Priests used hundreds of yards of linen to wrap the body up tight. Warm resin—a sticky substance derived from plants and trees—was applied between layers of linen to make it all stick together.

STEP 4. FINAL REST: A finished mummy might be placed in a stone or wood coffin called a sarcophagus. It could be carved or painted to resemble what the dead person inside looked like when alive.

KING TUT'S TOMB

Scientists used a digital version of King Tut's skull to create this model of what the boy king may have looked like in real life.

When Howard Carter discovered the tomb in 1922, the name King Tutankhamun became known around the world.

Born in approximately 1341 B.C., King Tut gained the throne in 1333, when he was only eight or nine years old. Because he was so young, advisors helped him rule. He was married to his half sister, the princess Ankhesenamun.

Tut's father, Akhenaten, replaced the deities that Egyptians had worshipped for centuries with a single sun god named Aten. He tried to erase inscriptions and imagery of the old gods wherever they could be found. When Tut became pharaoh, he decreed that the temples should be restored, along with the worship of Amun—which made his subjects happy.

That's about all Tut had time to do. About nine years into his reign, the young king suddenly died. There are many theories surrounding his death. Scientists who studied the mummy in 2010 found evidence of malaria, a disease spread by mosquitoes, and a bone disease. Other experts say there's evidence of massive trauma, perhaps due to a chariot crash. Though his death remains a mystery, King Tut is still one of the most famous mummies ever discovered in Egypt.

ANCIENT TREASURES

TUT'S JEWELS

King Tut's tomb was overflowing with thousands of treasures and artifacts for the pharaoh to use in the afterlife, which took Howard Carter's team more than ten years to catalog. Here's a look at just some of the amazing items Carter's team found:

1. USHABTI FIGURE: The tomb contained 431 statues of the king, called ushabti. They were meant to help Tut in the afterlife.

2. CANOPIC CHEST: This canopic chest held Tut's internal organs and was protected by a statue of the goddess Selket.

3. TUT'S BED: The feet of Tut's royal bed are cat feet!

4. TUT'S THRONE: The pharaoh's royal throne has a wood base, and is covered with gold, ivory, ebony, precious gems, and colored glass.

FIND THIS USHABTI FIGURE IN THE TEMPLE RUN GAME!

1

2

3

4

Tut's face was most likely clean-shaven in real life. All pharaohs, even females, wore a false, braided beard. This might have been a symbol that showed the pharaoh's connection to the gods.

The cobra and vulture on the headdress are symbols of protection.

King Tut's mummy was well protected inside three coffins. The outer two were made of wood frames covered with gold, and the inner was made of solid gold. A spectacular gold mask covered the mummy's face.

THE MUMMY'S CURSE?

It was the top story around the world. Lord Carnarvon, a key member of Howard Carter's team and sponsor of the dig, died just months after entering King Tut's burial chamber in November 1922.

Because Carnarvon's death happened so close to the opening of the tomb, stories of a curse exploded. Some even said the ancient Egyptians had put a magical curse on the tomb to protect it from grave robbers.

It turns out Carnarvon died because a mosquito bit him on the cheek and he cut the bite while shaving. The wound became infected.

In the end, it seems the curse was just a way to sell newspapers. Archaeologists found no evidence that the ancient Egyptians used curses to keep their tombs safe. But people today still like to speculate whether the curse was real.

THE NILE

As much as you want to stay and explore, you know Scarlett is right—you've got to get moving. Giza is on the banks of the Nile River, and as you approach the water you see boats traveling up and down the river.

Scarlett approaches a man on the shore standing next to a small wooden boat with a sail. She fishes something out of her pack, and seconds later you see a gold coin flashing in the sunlight. The man's eyes widen as he takes the coin. "Hop in. I hope you've got strong arms," he says.

AT ABOUT 4,132 MILES (6,650 KM) LONG, THE NILE IS THE LONGEST RIVER IN THE WORLD.

TRAVELING THE RIVER

Think of the Nile as a highway connecting the cities in ancient Egypt. As a result, the Egyptian people became expert boatmakers, and their craft improved with the ages.

Egyptians used boats for many reasons: for transportation, to carry goods, for fishing, for war, and just for fun. The first boats were simple rafts made of papyrus, a plant with tall stems. They evolved into crafts that were more boat-shaped, but these boats weren't strong enough to carry heavy goods up and down the river.

The next boats were made of wood, with flat bottoms. A single mast in the center of the boat would hold the sail, and a large rudder in the back was used to steer the boat. Egyptians used wood from acacia trees and cedar wood from Lebanon to build their watercrafts.

THE NILE FLOWS NORTHWARD FROM NORTHEASTERN AFRICA TO THE MEDITERRANEAN SEA.

Boats were sometimes put in tombs to help carry the dead to the afterlife.

DURING ANCIENT TIMES, EVERY YEAR FROM JUNE TO OCTOBER, THE RIVER WOULD FLOOD. WHEN THE WATER RETREATED, IT LEFT RICH SOIL PERFECT FOR GROWING CROPS LIKE WHEAT AND FLAX.

FARMING THE LAND

If you were traveling down the Nile in 1250 B.C., you would see farmers working in the soil by the river. These farmers worked for the pharaoh and would get paid with food, clothes, and shelter.

Farmers grew crops including wheat, barley, flax, figs, and other fruits and vegetables. Some of the grains they grew were used to feed farm animals. Raising livestock such as poultry and goats helped put food on the table, and oxen and cows pulled plows during planting time.

After a long day in the fields, most farmers would retreat to a simple house made of mud. Wealthier farmers had sturdier homes made of stone.

SACRED ANIMALS

The long trip downriver goes quickly as you take in the sights. You dip your oar into the water when something catches your eye up ahead—a huge, gray head slowly rising out of the water. "Cool!" you yell. "A hippo!"

The hippopotamus opens its mouth, revealing huge jaws and two long, sharp bottom teeth.

"Not cool," says Scarlett. "Hippos can be dangerous. That one there could easily topple this boat."

"So what do we do?" you ask, your heart suddenly pounding.

Scarlett grins. "Row faster!" The hippo lets out a loud roar.

You obey, rowing with all your might until the hippopotamus is out of sight.

After a hippo eats, the food stays in its stomach and ferments before it is digested.

HIPPOPOTAMUS

TYPE: Mammal

HABITAT: Rivers, swamps, and grasslands

SIZE: More than 15 feet (4.6 m) long, weighs up to 8,000 pounds (3,629 kg)

DIET: Herbivorous

LIFE SPAN: Up to 40 years

ANCIENT SYMBOL: Thought to represent Tauret, a fertility goddess

Hippos use their sense of smell to recognize each other.

EGYPT
1250 B.C.

Crocodiles don't often use their webbed feet for swimming.

NILE CROCODILE

TYPE: Reptile

HABITAT: Rivers, marshes, and swamps

SIZE: Up to 20 feet (6 m) long, weighs up to 1,650 pounds (748 kg)

DIET: Carnivorous

LIFE SPAN: Up to 45 years

ANCIENT SYMBOL: Worshipped as the god Sobek in hopes that crocodiles would stop attacking humans

A crocodile's snout is long and narrow, whereas an alligator's is more rounded.

SCARAB BEETLE
Also known as a dung beetle, Egyptians believed this beetle symbolized the god Khepri, who rolled the sun across the sky each day—mimicking the way that the scarab rolls a ball of dung across the desert sand.

JACKAL
This omnivorous canine scavenges for its food and will eat rotting meat. Ancient Egyptians noticed this, and the fact that they liked to hang out around cemeteries, so they associated the jackal with Anubis, a god of the underworld.

CAT
Felines were important to the Egyptians because they hunted pests such as rats and mice that ate precious grain. They are represented by the goddess Bast, who was pictured as a cat, or a woman with the head of a cat.

THE ROYAL CITY

Looking up, you find yourself in another busy city. You can see the tall pillars of temples not far from the shore.

"How did you know we should come to Thebes?" you ask Scarlett.

"Many pharaohs have made this city their capital," she tells you. "And then there's the ram's head on your device. It's a symbol of the god Amun-Re. There's a huge temple here dedicated to him."

You notice that the red light on your watch is blinking faintly. "Good guess!" you say.

A long avenue connects the Karnak temple to another temple for Amun-Re, the Luxor temple.

THE TEMPLE OF AMUN-RE AT KARNAK

Karnak is actually a site for three ancient temples: one dedicated to Mut, Amun-Re's wife, another to Montu, a warrior god, and the largest to Amun, the "king of the gods." Amun's temple was the largest in all of Egypt. Pharaoh after pharaoh rebuilt and enlarged it over 1,200 years. It even had a zoo!

But perhaps the most impressive feature of Amun's temple is the hypostyle hall. A hypostyle is a building whose roof is supported by pillars or columns. The hall is 54,000 square feet (5,017 sq m) in size, with twelve 80-foot (24-m)-high columns that once held up the roof. Dozens of smaller columns form magnificent aisles—a place worthy for the king of the gods!

EGYPT
1250 B.C.

A scene from *Transformers: Revenge of the Fallen* takes place in the hypostyle hall of Amun-Re's temple at Karnak.

TEMPLE STATS

BUILT: In sections, between 1500 B.C. and about 332 B.C.

LOCATION: Thebes, Egypt (modern-day Luxor), along the banks of the Nile River

DEDICATED TO: Amun-Re. Amun was worshipped as king of the gods, and he became known as Amun-Re after he was associated with Re, the sun god. He was important to many pharaohs.

WHO MADE IT: Over the centuries, slaves added to the temple under the direction of many pharaohs.

The homing beacon on your watch leads you right to the hypostyle hall, where you find a round turquoise-colored gem glistening in one of the pillars.

As you reach out to grab it, you hear an eerie cry. The demon monkeys have found you!

"Don't worry, kid," Scarlett says. "I'll get them to follow me. Go find a safe place to transport."

Scarlett runs before you can say another word and leads the demon monkeys away. You hate to leave her behind, but you know you have no choice.

When you activate the idol, a symbol appears on the fourth circle of the disc: a crude drawing of an owl. You have no idea where you're going—but you'll find out soon enough.

< MEET AN EXPLORER >

SARAH PARCAK
EGYPTOLOGIST

UNCOVERING EGYPT'S SECRETS

EXPLORER STATS

NAME: Sarah Parcak

MISSION: To find archaeological sites and features that allow us to ask better questions about the past, so that people around the world start caring more about our history.

HOME BASE: University of Alabama at Birmingham

CURRENT PROJECT: Mapping patterns of archaeological sites in Egypt, and looking at where sites are being threatened either by bulldozers or gangs digging up objects to sell on the black market.

FUN FACT: Sarah travels a lot, and to pass the time on long trips, she loves to play Temple Run!

Like the tombs of ancient kings, the landscape of modern Egypt holds many secrets. Buried under layers of sand, earth, and modern towns are the remnants of ancient settlements, tombs, and even pyramids. But how do you locate structures that have been buried for thousands of years? Sarah Parcak, a landscape architect who specializes in ancient Egypt, is using modern technology to find the answers.

Parcak studies high-resolution satellite imagery to look for variations in the geology of the Egyptian landscape. Since 2001, she has identified 17 potential pyramids, more than 1,000 tombs, and 3,000 settlements.

The Power of Satellites

Parcak's work began when she was an undergraduate at Yale. "My grandfather was a forestry professor at the University of Maine, and he was one of the first people to use aerial photography for forestry. I thought, wouldn't it be neat to figure out the modern version of what Grampy did?"

So Parcak started looking at satellite imagery of Egypt. "Let's say you're looking at a digital picture of someone's nose. You'd see pictures that are kind of close in color but somewhat different. But when you zoom out, you'd see that it's someone's nose."

Parcak isn't looking at noses, of course, but it's the same principle that allows her to identify pyramids and building foundations buried under layers of sand. One way she can identify underground structures is by looking at patterns of vegetation growth. "Roots can't go through stone, so vegetation growth is going to be stunted," she explains.

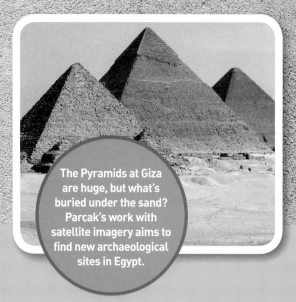

The Pyramids at Giza are huge, but what's buried under the sand? Parcak's work with satellite imagery aims to find new archaeological sites in Egypt.

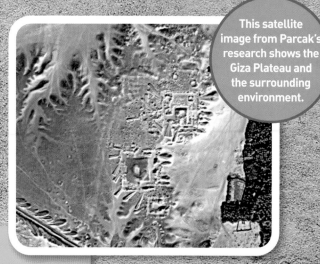

This satellite image from Parcak's research shows the Giza Plateau and the surrounding environment.

"Then you use computer algorithms to detect changes in vegetation health."

Then, Parcak looks for 12 specific features that will tell her if what she's looking at might be a pyramid. For example, the size of the object is one thing she looks for. She knows that ancient pyramids would be 164 by 164 feet (50 by 50 m). If the structure matches 11 of those 12 features, "we can say it's probably a pyramid. At the end of the day you have to excavate and see what's there."

"What's exciting to me is the more work I do, the more I realize that there is to be found," Parcak says. "This is just the tip of the iceberg."

KEEPING SITES SAFE

The next step for Parcak will be to excavate one of the sites she has discovered. The Egyptian government allows archaeologists to work on only one site. "Once you pick the site, that's where you need to work," so Parcak will have to rely on her data to make a good choice.

Parcak has another concern: robbers who dig up ancient sites illegally and steal their treasures. Looting has been happening in Egypt for thousands of years, but the problem has worsened in recent years due to government upheaval. Archaeologists are reporting seeing pits in the sand, dug by looters breaking into underground tombs.

"I have to be careful with my data because there are so many looters around," she says. Luckily, "the majority of sites are actually underneath modern towns, so they're safe."

Parcak's research has uncovered lots of new details about Egyptian structures, like these sharp details in mortuary architecture from this pyramid complex in South Saqqara.

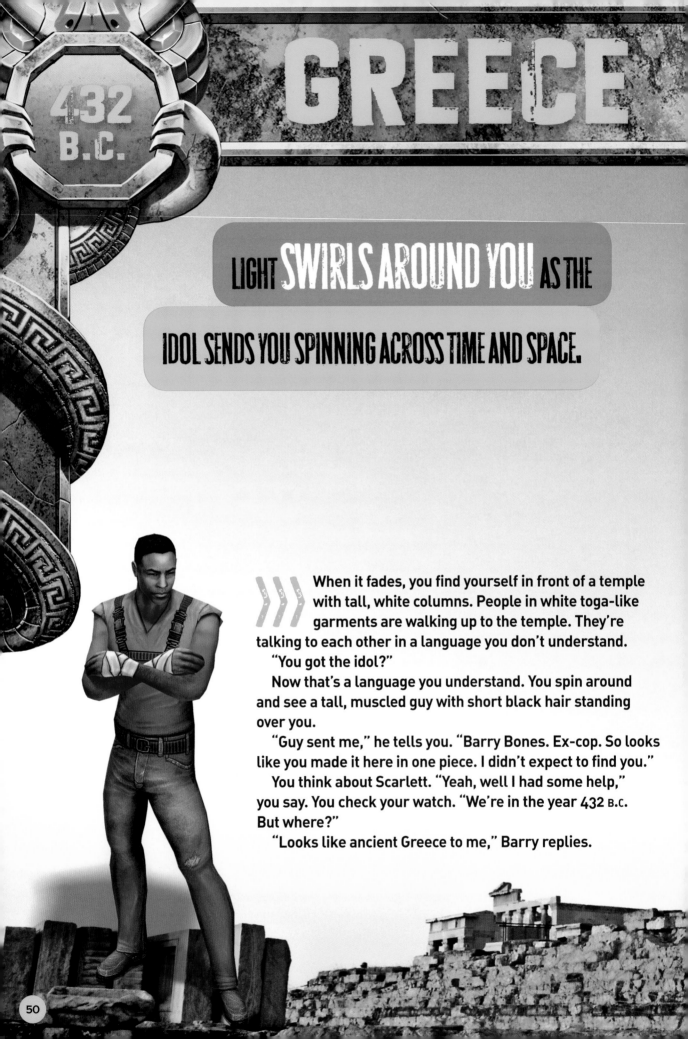

432 B.C.

LIGHT SWIRLS AROUND YOU AS THE IDOL SENDS YOU SPINNING ACROSS TIME AND SPACE.

>>> When it fades, you find yourself in front of a temple with tall, white columns. People in white toga-like garments are walking up to the temple. They're talking to each other in a language you don't understand.

"You got the idol?"

Now that's a language you understand. You spin around and see a tall, muscled guy with short black hair standing over you.

"Guy sent me," he tells you. "Barry Bones. Ex-cop. So looks like you made it here in one piece. I didn't expect to find you."

You think about Scarlett. "Yeah, well I had some help," you say. You check your watch. "We're in the year 432 B.C. But where?"

"Looks like ancient Greece to me," Barry replies.

Europe
GREECE

ALBANIA MACEDONIA
GREECE TURKEY
PERSIAN
KINGDOM
Athens
MEDITERRANEAN
SEA
☐ Athens and Allies 432 B.C.

BLACK SEA

▲ Mt. Olympus
GREECE

IONIAN
SEA

AEGEAN
SEA

Parthenon
● Athens
● Olympia

SEA OF CRETE

Crete

MEDITERRANEAN
SEA

0   100   200 miles
0   100   200 kilometers

THE PARTHENON

The red light on your watch is blinking.

"The gem is probably in that big temple over there," you say. "But it's pretty crowded here. Pretty soon somebody's going to notice we look different."

Barry throws a crumpled-up white garment at you. "Here's a chiton for you," he says. It's the same thing the ancient Greeks are wearing.

"Thanks," you say. "What about you?" Barry is wearing a blue t-shirt and worn jeans.

He laughs. "Nobody's gonna mess with me."

THERE ARE TWO ROOMS INSIDE THE PARTHENON. THE BIGGER ONE, CALLED THE NAOS, HELD THE STATUE OF ATHENA. THE SMALLER ROOM, THE OPISTHODOMOS, WAS USED AS A TREASURY.

The Parthenon is a temple built in the Doric style. Doric style columns are plain, sturdy columns that might taper slightly at the top.

THE LONG SIDE IS 228 FEET (70 M) LONG. THAT'S LONGER THAN FIVE SCHOOL BUSES!

TEMPLE STATS

BUILT: 447–432 B.C.

LOCATION: The Acropolis in Athens, Greece. An acropolis is a part of a city that is fortified against invaders, and usually sits on top of a hill.

DEDICATED TO: The goddess Athena and gets its name from the goddess's aspect as Athena Parthenos, which means "Athena the virgin"

WHO MADE IT: Pericles, a statesman who helped develop democracy in Athens; architects Ictinus and Callicrates; and Phidias, a sculptor who worked as the artistic director on the project

HONORING ATHENA

Even though there's a crowd of people heading for the temple, everyone is fairly quiet. You also notice that most people are standing outside the row of columns, looking in. Nobody is going inside.

"What's everyone looking at?" you wonder, as you and Barry make your way to the front of the crowd. Then you gasp.

Inside the temple is an enormous statue of a goddess. It's made of white marble with glistening accents. Then you notice that people in the crowd are murmuring the same name over and over.

"Athena."

Besides being a protector of Athens, Athena was also a goddess of weaving, pottery, heroes, and wisdom. One of her symbols is the watchful owl, which has come to be associated with Athena's wisdom.

LEGENDS OF ATHENA

1. CONTEST FOR ATHENS: According to legend, Athena and the god Poseidon argued over who should be able to found a city in Greece, so they had a contest to see who could give the city the best gift. Poseidon struck the ground with his trident to give the city water, but it turned out to be salt water. Athena created the first olive tree. She won, and the city was named after her.

2. THE FIRST SPIDER: When a young girl named Arachne bragged that her weaving talents were better than Athena's, the goddess became angry. She and Arachne had a weaving contest. Athena couldn't find anything wrong with Arachne's beautiful piece, which only made her angrier. She turned Arachne into a spider so she could weave forever.

3. HELPER OF HEROES: When Hercules was performing his twelve labors, Athena helped with three of them.

1

2

3

The helmet shows Athena's role as a wise counselor of war and defender of Athens.

The statue of Athena was removed from the Parthenon in the fifth century A.D. when the temple was converted into a Christian church. It does not exist today, but some smaller marble copies can be seen in museums. A full-size reproduction can be found at the Parthenon in Nashville, Tennessee, U.S.A. It's made of cement and gilded with gold flakes.

There is a snake on Athena's shield, and more snakes and the head of Medusa on her breastplate. In mythology, Athena is the one who transformed Medusa from a beautiful maiden into a monster.

In her right hand is Nike, a symbol of victory. It looks like she's holding it out to the citizens of Athens.

THE OLYMPIANS

The ancient Greeks worshipped 12 major gods and goddesses, who were thought to live on the peak of Mount Olympus.

APHRODITE: goddess of love and beauty

APOLLO: god of music, prophecy, and healing

ARES: god of war

ARTEMIS: goddess of hunting, wild animals, and childbirth

ATHENA: goddess of war, wisdom, and crafts

DEMETER: goddess of the harvest

DIONYSUS: god of wine and revelry

HEPHAESTUS: god of metalworking

HERA: goddess of women and marriage

HERMES: god of travel, thievery, and shepherds; messenger of the gods

POSEIDON: god of the sea and horses

ZEUS: king of the gods; god of the sky, weather, and law

TREASURES OF THE PARTHENON

Thomas Bruce, the seventh lord of Elgin, shown in this photograph from 1860, caused controversy after removing what are today known as the "Elgin Marbles" from Greece.

In 1687, the people of Venice attacked Athens. They stored gunpowder in the Parthenon, and a major explosion destroyed many of the sculptures that remained. So what happened to the rest of them?

In the early 1800s, Athens became part of the Ottoman Empire. The British ambassador to the empire, Thomas Bruce, or Lord Elgin, wanted to do something to save the sculptures. Claiming he had permission from the Ottoman authorities, he removed about half of the sculptures left and brought them back to Britain where they were later acquired by the British Museum. They've been on display there for free since 1816 and have come to be known as the "Elgin Marbles."

In the 1980s, the Greek government asked for the return of the artifacts. The British Museum has refused. The debate still rages as to whether Lord Elgin stole the artifacts without proper permission, or if he was genuinely trying to save a piece of history that could have been lost forever.

FIND THIS GREEK VASE IN THE TEMPLE RUN GAME!

ANCIENT TREASURES

PAINTED POTTERY

Some of the most common—and beautiful—artifacts from ancient Greece are painted pots. Artists used clay to make jugs, vases, cups, and other useful items. The earliest pots were painted with geometric shapes. More elaborate paintings showed scenes from daily life or mythology.

Archaeologists study the paintings on pots to learn about what life was like for the ancient Greeks. For example, a painting on one pot showed men plowing a field with oxen. Other pottery shows children playing with wheeled toys, young men training to be athletes, and women spinning wool into thread.

A frieze is a band of sculpture or painting that wraps around a building, usually along the top wall. The Parthenon had 524 feet (160 m) of friezes inside the outer columns. Today, the British Museum has about half of those friezes. This piece of the frieze shows two scenes: on the left, a priest and a child hold Athena's sacred robe. On the right, Athena sits on a stool and talks to Hephaestus, the god of metalwork.

This sculpture of Dionysus, the god of wine, was from the pediment under the roof of the Parthenon. Because pediments are triangle-shaped—wide at the bottom and narrow at the top—many of the sculpted figures were shown lying down or reclining.

The British Museum has 15 of the original 92 metopes (a type of frieze) from the Parthenon. This panel shows a story from mythology. Centaurs were mythical creatures with the lower body of a horse and upper body of a man. They were said to be fierce warriors. This sculpture shows a centaur battling a member of the human Lapith tribe from northern Greece.

This frieze shows a chariot race in action. High-speed chariot races took place at the Panathenaic Games (the ancient Olympics) in Athens. At the end of the race, the rider would leap off the chariot and finish on foot.

As the two of you walk, you can't help staring at the ancient Greeks around you. You find yourself wondering what their lives are like.

The homing beacon leads you to a yellow gem displayed prominently on one of the Doric columns. Making sure no one is looking, you reach for it.

"I feel kind of bad doing this," you say.

"Well, I used to be a cop, but I won't arrest you," Barry says. "These are special circumstances. You're saving the world from demon monkeys. Just don't go crazy."

> Our modern Olympic games are named after athletic contests held by the ancient Greeks that probably began in 776 B.C.

GREAT MOMENTS IN ANCIENT GREECE

776 B.C.
The first Olympic games were held. Only men were allowed to compete.

508 B.C.
Democracy began in Athens. Male citizens could vote on laws and elect politicians.

480 B.C.
The dawn of Greece's Classical Period, when arts, music, and theater flourished for almost 200 years.

479 B.C.
The Persians attacked Greece, but were defeated.

432 B.C.
The construction of the Parthenon was completed.

338 B.C.
Philip II of Macedonia conquered Athens. When he died, his son Alexander the Great ruled Greece.

146 B.C.
Greece became part of the Roman Empire.

SLAVES, WOMEN, AND CITIZENS

Life was pretty good in Athens if you were a citizen. If you were a slave or a woman, it was a different story.

SLAVES in Athens had no rights. Some were bought from other lands, and others were born slaves. Most enslaved people had to do the hardest jobs that nobody else wanted to do. Other slaves became nurses, teachers, or craftspeople.

A **WOMAN** born in Athens who was not a slave still wasn't a citizen. She couldn't vote or go to school. Girls were trained by their mothers to learn how to run a home and take care of children. Unless a woman was very poor, she probably had slaves to help her take care of these duties.

To be a **CITIZEN** of Athens, you had to be an Athenian-born male who was not a slave. You could vote and make decisions about what you wanted to do with your life. A male not born in Athens was not a citizen, but still had more freedom than women.

At its height, Athens had about 300,000 residents—and up to 100,000 of those residents were slaves.

You and Barry step away from the Athena worshippers so you can activate the portal. A symbol appears on the fifth circle: a Chinese character.

"Looks like we're going to China," you say, and then the light swallows up both of you as you transport.

CHINA

WHEN YOU LAND IN CHINA, IT'S SUNNY AND

A LITTLE BIT COOLER. YOU'RE AT THE BOTTOM OF A HILL.

>>> When you look up, you see a small army of Chinese workers building a long stone wall that snakes along the hilltop.

"Is that the Great Wall of China?" you ask.

"Sure looks like it," Barry says. "What do you want to bet that the gem is somewhere up there?"

You look at your watch. "Well, it's not down here. But won't we be kind of noticeable up there?"

Barry's expression darkens. "The emperors of China used slaves to build this wall," he says. "They won't want to do anything to draw the attention of the guards. We should be okay."

Asia
CHINA

0   400   800 miles
0   400   800 kilometers

〜〜〜 Great Wall,
       Qin Dynasty

CHINA

SEA OF
JAPAN

Beijing

YELLOW
SEA

Xi'an ●● Terra-
         Cotta
         Warriors

EAST
CHINA
SEA

▨ Qin Dynasty 221–206 B.C.

CHINA

SOUTH
CHINA SEA

PACIFIC OCEAN

THE GREAT WALL

With Barry at your side, you start to scale the banks of the hill leading up to the wall, hoping you won't be spotted. The workers are focused on their task of laying the bricks to build the wall, and the guards are focused on the workers.

"This is pretty cool," you tell Barry. "I mean, I learned about the Great Wall in school. Everybody knows about it. And we're seeing it built!"

"I guess you're right," Barry agrees. "The work that went into this thing is pretty amazing."

TODAY, THE LONGEST CONNECTED STRETCH OF THE GREAT WALL OF CHINA SNAKES ACROSS THE COUNTRY FOR ABOUT 5,500 MILES (8,850 KM).

BUILDING THE GREAT WALL OF CHINA

8TH CENTURY B.C.
China was made up of warring states controlled by warlords. These warlords built the first walls.

221 B.C.
China's first emperor, Qin Shi Huang, unified the country. He ordered the building of walls to connect the existing walls.

141 B.C.
Emperor Wudi of the Han dynasty ordered the strengthening of the wall as protection against the Xiongnu people, a large, wandering tribe.

121 B.C.
The wall was fortified with forts, towers, and castles.

A.D. 1206
During the Yuan dynasty, the Mongols controlled China. They had no interest in continuing to build the wall.

A.D. 1368
After the Mongols were defeated, the emperors of the Ming dynasty got back to work rebuilding and improving the wall.

A.D. 1487
Most of the wall that survives today results from the reign of the Ming dynasty emperor Hongzhi, who added strategic passes and gates to the wall.

A MASSIVE MARVEL

The wall took millions of workers and more than 2,000 years to build. Its purpose was to keep invaders out of China, especially the Mongols from the north. It isn't one long, continuous wall, however; there are large spaces between some parts of the wall. Natural barriers such as mountains were also used to connect parts of the wall.

The Great Wall is the longest structure on Earth made by humans.

Not all of the wall's pieces are connected. If you joined them together the wall would be more than 13,000 miles (20,920 km) long—more than four times the distance from New York to California.

GREAT WALL STATS

HEIGHT: On average most parts were about 25 feet (8 m) high.

BUILT WITH: Rocks; bricks made of earth or stone; and wooden boards. A sticky mixture made of rice was used to glue bricks together.

MYTH BUSTED!: You may have heard that the Great Wall can be seen from space. That's not true. Weather patterns, plus the fact that the wall is made from materials whose colors are similar to those of its surroundings, make the wall nearly impossible to view from orbit.

A.D. 1644
The Ming dynasty ended, and the emperors of the Manchu dynasty tried a new strategy of trying to make peace with their neighbors. It worked out pretty well, and repairs on the wall mostly stopped as a result.

MEET THE EMPERORS

The light on your homing beacon is flashing faintly, so you and Barry climb up near a finished part of the wall.

Something you read in school comes back to you. "I wonder if these guys are working for Emperor Qin. He's the first emperor to start building the wall."

Suddenly, you hear a familiar cry.

"*Aaaaaiiiiieeeeeeeeee!*"

The demon monkeys are here! In ancient China! You see their glowing red eyes as they charge up the hill toward you.

Barry nods to some bamboo scaffolding leaning up against the wall. "Let's climb!"

You hurry up the wall and soon you're 25 feet (8 m) in the air, racing for your life.

> Qin Shi Huang wanted to rule forever, so he often tried pills and potions for lengthening his life. He even sent his servants to look for mythical islands where, according to legend, magic herbs grew.

EMPEROR QIN SHI HUANG

Born Zhao Zheng in 259 B.C., he was 13 years old when he was named to the throne of the Qin state in northern China. In 221 B.C. he unified the warring states into one state, the Qin state. He gave himself the name Shihuangdi, which means "first sovereign emperor." From then on, he was known as Qin Shi Huang. He achieved many great things during his reign, such as constructing a 3,000-mile (4,828-km) wall to protect the land from invaders—the beginning of the Great Wall. He also standardized weights and measures, laws, and written language and created a national currency. Plus, he ordered construction of many roads and canals.

Confucius was a philosopher who was born in 551 B.C. Many people in Asia still celebrate his birthday on September 28.

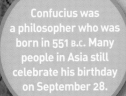

EMPEROR WUDI

Born Liu Che, he was the 11th son of the fifth emperor of the Han dynasty, Jingdi, according to historians. He reigned from 141 B.C. until his death in 87 B.C.

During his reign, he expanded China's empire through force, added hundreds of miles to the Great Wall, and repaired the existing one. But his most lasting contribution might have been making Confucianism the official religion of China. Confucianism is a system of teachings that sets down rules for being a good person. For example, children are taught to respect their parents. It was prevalent in China for more than 2,000 years.

EMPEROR HONGZHI

Hongzhi's reign as an emperor of the Ming dynasty from A.D. 1487 to 1505 was dubbed the "Hongzhi Silver Age." Hongzhi was known for being a smart student and for his peaceful ways of governing. Like other emperors of the Ming dynasty, he was responsible for building many parts of the Great Wall.

< EXPLORE >
THE TERRA-COTTA ARMY

Emperor Qin Shi Huang ordered many great building projects during his rule. Besides starting construction of the Great Wall, it is believed that his capital city had more than 270 palaces. But his most astonishing achievement is his massive tomb complex, which contains an army of warriors ready to defend him in the afterlife. It took more than 700,000 workers to create the massive tomb, which is still being excavated today.

Archaeologists estimate there are about 8,000 terra-cotta figures guarding the tomb, like this kneeling archer.

ANCIENT TREASURES

TOOLS FOR THE AFTERLIFE

The chambers contained many artifacts and treasures, including objects made of jade; iron farm tools; and weapons such as bows, arrows, swords, and spears. Ancient historian Sima Qian claimed that the tomb was booby-trapped to protect the treasures inside. Crossbows were triggered to automatically release arrows if an intruder entered.

FIND THIS JADE TREASURE IN THE TEMPLE RUN GAME!

An army of life-size warriors and horses guards the tomb. They are made of terra-cotta and each one has a unique face.

The army is facing east—the direction that the emperor's enemies came from when he was alive.

Bright paint once decorated the statues, but that has faded over time.

A LONG-KEPT SECRET

The underground tomb stayed hidden for more than 2,000 years. Then, in 1974, some farmers were digging a well in the Shaanxi Province near the city of Xi'an, China, when they discovered an underground chamber and pieces of a clay figure. Archaeologists were brought in, and in a dig that has lasted decades they uncovered about 600 pits containing the soldiers.

The pits where the army is stored are near the actual tomb of Qin Shi Huang, which has not been excavated out of respect for the ancient emperor. But a historian named Sima Qian, who lived from 145 to 87 B.C., wrote about how the emperor's tomb was made to look like a replica of the emperor's kingdom, with pearls set on the ceiling like stars, and golden birds sitting in pine trees carved from jade.

ANIMAL SYMBOLS

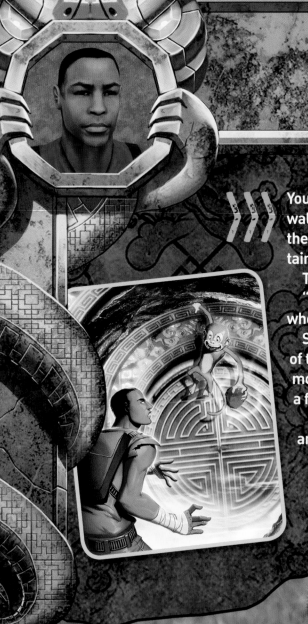

Your heart pounds as you race across the top of the wall. Then Barry swings from a tree branch, jumps off the wall, and heads for a cave in the side of the mountain. You catch up to him in the cave, breathing heavily.

Then you notice the red light blinking on your watch. "It's the beacon!" you cry. "Is the gem in here somewhere?"

Suddenly, you see two eyes glowing at the entrance of the cave. A monkey enters—but it isn't a demon monkey. Its fur shines gold in the firelight, and it has a funny, pushed-in face.

The monkey walks up to you and opens up a paw—and inside is a glittering, ruby red gem.

Today, mainly due to a disappearing habitat, giant pandas are considered an endangered species, meaning they are in serious danger of becoming extinct.

Giant pandas cannot walk on their hind legs like other species of bears.

A panda has a large wrist bone that acts almost like a thumb, helping it grip food.

GIANT PANDA

TYPE: Mammal

HABITAT: Bamboo forests in the mountains

SIZE: Up to 5 feet (1.5 m) long, weighs up to 330 pounds (150 kg)

DIET: Bamboo leaves, shoots, and stems

SYMBOLISM: Pandas have always been very special to the Chinese people. They are said to represent peace.

CHINA
221 B.C.

Its flat face might have developed as a protection against the cold. A nose that stuck out more, without fur to protect it, would be more likely to get frostbite.

The color of a male's fur is more orange than that of a female monkey.

The monkey's thick fur helps keep it warm during freezing winters in the mountains.

GOLDEN SNUB-NOSED MONKEY

TYPE: Mammal

HABITAT: Forests in the mountains

SIZE: Up to 30 inches (76 cm) long (not including the tail), weighs up to 86 pounds (39 kg)

DIET: Lichens, trees, shrubs, vines, and some insects

SYMBOLISM: In the tradition of the Chinese zodiac, people born under the sign of the monkey are clever, energetic, positive, and charming.

The monkey quickly leaves, and you're left staring at the gem in disbelief.

"What are you waiting for?" Barry asks. "Let's get out of here."

You place the gem in the idol, and a new symbol appears in one of the circles. It's a drawing of a flower with six petals.

"That could be anywhere," you say.

"But anywhere is where we need to be," Barry says. "Let's do this!"

PETRA

THE IDOL TRANSPORTS YOU TO A GORGE

WITH BEAUTIFUL SANDSTONE CLIFFS

RISING ON EITHER SIDE OF YOU.

>>> It's hot, and a bright sun shines in the blue sky overhead.

"Is there a temple somewhere around here?" you ask. The homing beacon on your watch isn't even blinking.

Barry grins. "I know this place," he says. "It's pretty awesome. Follow me."

"Aw, come on," you plead. "Why don't you just tell me?" But Barry just keeps smiling and walks ahead of you.

JORDAN

MEDITERRANEAN SEA

Amman

DEAD
SEA

JORDAN

Petra
Wadi Musa

JORDAN   Asia

0   50   100 miles
0   50   100 kilometers

CLIFF CITY

Barry leads you for what feels like a mile through the narrow gorge. The pathway is crowded with other travelers. Some are leading camels, and others are pulling carts. Everyone is chatting noisily.

When you finally emerge, you are stunned by an amazing sight. You're in the middle of a valley, with red sandstone cliffs rising up around you. But that's not what's amazing. What looks to be an entire city has been carved right into the rocky cliffs!

If you visit Jordan today, you are not allowed to bring a motorized vehicle into Petra. Tourists can ride in horse-drawn carts.

MEET THE NABATAEANS

How did a place in the middle of a desert become so important?

The credit goes to the Nabataeans, an Arab tribe who made the city their capital sometime in the first century B.C. The key to their success was their ability to harness water. They used a system of tanks, pipes, pools, and waterways to capture and transport rainwater and water from nearby springs. Archaeologists think they may have harnessed 12 million gallons (45 million L) of water a day—enough to serve the needs of 100,000 people.

Archaeologists don't know much about what the Nabataeans were like before they came to Petra. It is believed they were nomads who wandered the desert. Some would say it was impossible for a nomadic tribe to build a sophisticated city in the desert—but the proof remains, carved into the sandstone walls.

PETRA
1 B.C.

Petra is located in the valley where it is believed that Moses, the leader of the Israelites, performed a miracle. He struck a rock with his staff and water sprang out.

Scenes from *Indiana Jones and the Last Crusade* were filmed in Petra.

TOMB STATS

KNOWN AS: Corinthian Tomb

BUILT: Between A.D. 40 and 70

LOCATION: Petra, near the western border of Jordan

WHO MADE IT: It was built during the reign of the Nabataean king Malichus II.

SPECIAL FEATURE: There are four water basins carved into the front, which are believed to have been used for cleansing rituals.

A CENTER OF TRADE

At its height, Petra was the prosperous center of the Arab world. The city was in the center of two big trade routes. It could offer water, food, and rest for the traders who were passing through. Traders from such places as China, Egypt, and India traveled here to sell their wares: spices, fabrics, precious metals, and other goods.

Between 10,000 and 30,000 people lived in Petra. They would have made their living providing food and shelter to the visiting traders.

For centuries, Petra was a secret to the western world. In 1812, a Swiss explorer named Johann Ludwig Burckhardt became the first European in modern times to see the city. He passed through the gorge leading to Petra—called the Siq—disguised in Arabic clothing.

‹ EXPLORE ›
THE BUILDINGS OF PETRA

How did the Nabataeans carve such complicated structures, like the famous Treasury building, out of the rock? Researcher Dr. Shaher Rababeh thinks he has found the answer.
To build the Treasury, carvers climbed up the rocky mountain path until they got to where the top of the building would be. They carved steps into the rock to make their movement easier. Then they carved a ledge across the rock where the building would stand. They stood on the ledge and carved from the top down, removing traces of each ledge until they got to the ground.

Romans conquered the Nabataeans in A.D. 106, but Petra thrived as a trading center for a few centuries after that. Many of Petra's buildings, such as the Treasury pictured here, still stand today, but experts believe earthquakes may have ultimately led to the city being abandoned.

THE MONASTERY: You'll have to climb up 800 steps to see Al-Deir, "the monastery," an unfinished tomb. In the Byzantine era in the first century A.D., this building was used as a church.

It is believed that these sculptures were of gods and goddesses. Some people think they may have been defaced in medieval times by those who thought them to be offensive.

The tomb is almost 128 feet (39 m) high.

THE TREASURY:
This building is actually a tomb that was named Al Khazneh, which means "the treasury" in Arabic. It got its name from legends that pirates hid a treasure in an urn on the second level.

THE ROMAN THEATER:
This Roman-style outdoor theater could seat more than 8,000 people. It was built before the Roman invasion but was then redesigned.

DESERT ANIMALS

The homing beacon on your watch begins to blink. You follow the signal through the crowded streets. Camels thirstily drink from troughs in the street. The air smells of incense and cooked meat. Barry stops at a man hovered over an open fire, hands over some coins, and comes back with two pieces of flatbread with some charred meat stuffed inside. You wonder what kind of meat it is . . .

"Better than a taco," he says, handing one to you. "Time travelers gotta remember to eat when the opportunity presents itself."

A Bactrian camel has two humps; an Arabian camel has one.

Nostrils can squeeze shut to keep out blowing sand, and the camel's eyelashes are extra heavy for the same reason.

Camels can go several weeks without water if they eat enough moisture-containing plants.

BACTRIAN CAMEL

TYPE: Mammal

HABITAT: Deserts

SIZE: Over 7 feet (2.1 m) tall at the hump, weighs up to about 1,300 pounds (590 kg)

DIET: Herbivorous

ANCIENT USES: Transportation; hides were used to make tents; milk and meat; dung could be used for fuel.

ARABIAN ORYX

TYPE: Mammal

HABITAT: Gravel plains, savannas, and deserts

SIZE: Up to 4.5 feet (1.4 m) tall, weighs up to 463 pounds (210 kg)

DIET: Herbivorous

LIFE SPAN: 20 years

ANCIENT USES: The Bedouin people of the desert hunted oryx for their meat and hides.

Arabian oryx can live for long periods on the water found in plants. The oryx is also said to have the ability to find water sources from miles away.

The Arabian oryx is the national animal of Jordan. A member of the antelope family, it is smaller than other oryxes, with white fur.

It is believed that the Arabian oryx started the legend of the unicorn. When you see it from the side, it looks like it has only one horn growing from its head.

 The homing beacon leads you to one of the buildings carved into the side of the rock. You see a rosy pink gem inside the carving of the flower, and you carefully put the gem in the idol.

"On to the next place," you tell Barry.

"I'm gonna hang out here for a while," he says. "But you'll do all right without me."

< MEET AN EXPLORER >

ANDREW M. SMITH II
ARCHAEOLOGIST

EXPLORER STATS

NAME: Andrew M. Smith II

MISSION: To understand, from a rural perspective, the role of Petra in the ancient and modern economy and to examine how the city evolved in antiquity

HOME BASE: The George Washington University in Washington, D.C., U.S.A.

CURRENT PROJECT: Examining all forms of economic activity in remote areas of Petra, like Bir Madhkur, which was a hub of rural settlement and a center for interaction between farmers, herders, soldiers, and merchants

WHY HE BECAME AN ARCHAEOLO-GIST: Smith spent a summer on an archaeological dig at a Roman fort in Jordan. He lived in tents in the desert and remembers walking into the fort under a full moon.

FINDING THE ROADS TO PETRA

Archaeologist Andrew M. Smith II believes that one way to learn about ancient Petra is to study the area around it.

"I'm very interested in the fact that if you're going to understand how Petra evolved in the city, you really have to look at the population outside the city," he says.

That's why, since 2008, he has led expeditions to explore the roads and trade routes outside Petra. He has focused on the area of Wadi Araba, which is west of Petra and borders Israel and Jordan. The incense trade routes have been well documented in Israel, but not in Jordan, and Smith and his team were looking for that "missing link."

Missing Link Found

In the summer of 2013, Smith's team made an important discovery: the ruins of a caravan station on the route from Petra to Gaza. They found a 98-by-98-foot (30-by-30-m) structure that contained a kitchen, with ovens and a shelf. Pottery and coins found at the site date it to the first century A.D.

"There were a bunch of people living here and working here," Smith explains. "Now it just looks like a bunch of ruins, but you have to imagine it was a really busy truck stop."

Exploring caravan sites like this one reminds Smith of his childhood.

"When I was a kid in North Carolina, we would go out and find ruins of old houses, and that's basically what you find," he says. "You find these old foundations and tons and tons of pottery."

Smith describes his excavation to onlookers of the northwest tower of a Roman fort at Bir Madhkur near Petra.

Smith walks among the rubble at the ancient Roman fort of Da'janiya in Jordan. He first went there as a student, and it was the first site he ever worked at.

WORKING WITH THE BEDOUIN

The Bedouin people are nomadic desert dwellers of the Middle East. Several years ago Smith began working with the Bedouin of Jordan, who helped his discoveries by leading his team to old ruins.

"They know what they're looking for and are eager to help us," Smith says.

When Smith excavated the caravan station, he hired Bedouin to help on his team, along with students. One of his goals is to help the Bedouin by reviving the incense trade and bringing tourists outside of Petra into the outlying areas.

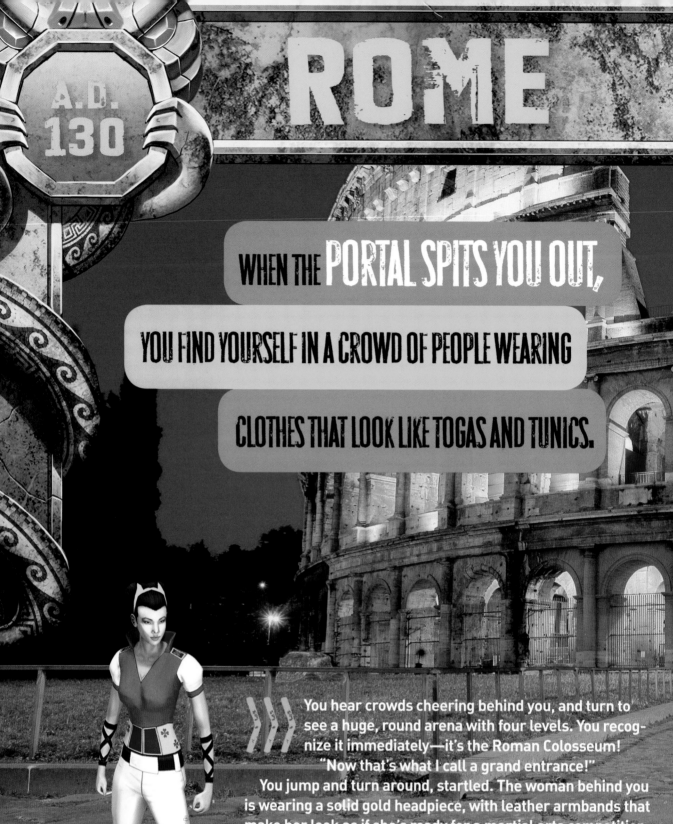

ROME

WHEN THE PORTAL SPITS YOU OUT,

YOU FIND YOURSELF IN A CROWD OF PEOPLE WEARING

CLOTHES THAT LOOK LIKE TOGAS AND TUNICS.

You hear crowds cheering behind you, and turn to see a huge, round arena with four levels. You recognize it immediately—it's the Roman Colosseum!

"Now that's what I call a grand entrance!"

You jump and turn around, startled. The woman behind you is wearing a solid gold headpiece, with leather armbands that make her look as if she's ready for a martial arts competition.

"Who are you?" you ask.

"Karma Lee," she replies. "Barry Bones sent me from the future. It's a time travel thing."

You look down at your watch. The homing beacon isn't flashing.

"I'd love to watch the races, but I guess we need to find a temple and the next gem," you say.

"Well, let's see what we find," Karma suggests.

ITALY

Europe
ITALY

Hadrian's Wall
BRITANNIA
GERMANIA
Europe
Rome
ITALIA
Asia
Africa

Greatest Extent of the Roman Empire

ITALY
TIBER RIVER
Rome — Pantheon
Colosseum
ADRIATIC SEA
TYRRHENIAN SEA
IONIAN SEA
SICILY ▲ Mt. Olympus
MEDITERRANEAN SEA

0   100   200 miles
0 100 200 kilometers

CONSTRUCTING THE PANTHEON

">>> "My watch says it's A.D. 130. So it's not as ancient as some of the other places I've been," you tell Karma.

"Sounds like you've been around," the explorer says.

You nod. "I can hardly believe it."

The two of you start walking through the crowded streets of Rome. Before long, your watch starts to beep. You follow the signal to a tall building with columns across the front.

"Looks like we found the Pantheon," says Karma.

"Is it a temple?" you ask.

Karma laughs. "I'll bet you my black belt it is!"

Each column weighs 60 tons (54 MT).

A BRIEF HISTORY OF ANCIENT ROME

753 B.C.
City was founded.

509 B.C.
Rome became a republic governed by a Senate.

44 B.C.
Rome's great general, Julius Caesar, died.

27 B.C.
Augustus became Rome's first emperor.

A.D. 64
Fire destroyed much of the city.

A.D. 122
Emperor Hadrian began construction of a huge wall to protect the British territory.

A.D. 395
Rome was split into two empires—east and west.

A.D. 410
City was attacked and taken by the Visigoths, a tribe of Germanic people.

A.D. 476
End of the Roman Empire

THE DOME IS ABOUT 142 FEET (43 M) IN DIAMETER, AND 72 FEET (22 M) FROM ITS BASE TO THE VERY TOP.

For centuries, the triangular pediment contained a sculpture showing the battle of the Titans, giant-size gods from Roman and Greek mythology. The sculpture was lost when the temple was rebuilt.

M·AGRIPPA·L·F·COS·TERTIVM·FECIT

TEMPLE STATS

BUILT IN: A.D. 27

WHO MADE IT: Marcus Vipsanius Agrippa, who was a deputy to Augustus, the first emperor of Rome. He oversaw buildings and public works.

WHO REBUILT IT: About 100 years later, after it had caught fire twice, it was completely rebuilt by the emperor Hadrian.

WHAT IT MEANS: A pantheon is a group of all the gods belonging to one religion. Most temples were dedicated to just one god or goddess, but it is believed that the Pantheon was built to honor all of them.

THE OCULUS

The main part of the temple is a huge dome made of concrete. In the center of the dome is a 27-foot (8-m) circular opening called an oculus. It lets a lot of light into the temple. When it rains, the water falls to the slightly slanted floor and leaves the temple through drainpipes. The walls of the temple are lined with colored marble, and the domed ceiling was likely decorated with bronze and elaborate molding. The structure has inspired architects throughout the ages.

"You know, the Romans built their temples all over," Karma tells you, as if she's teaching her favorite class. "I've been to some of them. Some are up north in England, and you can find them in the Middle East, too. Rome was a pretty big empire at one time. But the Pantheon is right here in Rome."

That gets you thinking. "Rome must have had some pretty powerful leaders to grow their empire so big." Karma nods. "You can say that again."

JULIUS CAESAR
HE MADE ROME A GREAT EMPIRE

He may have died more than 2,000 years ago, but his name and his achievements haven't faded with time.

Caesar was born some time around the year 100 B.C. to a noble family. As a young man he started a life of politics and military service. In 59 B.C., he was elected a consul of Rome—one of two leaders who ruled the Roman republic, along with the Senate. As a general of the Roman army, he won many battles and expanded the empire. He emerged victorious in a Roman civil war and became a dictator of the Roman Empire: a single ruler who held all of the power in his hands.

Unhappy with Caesar's dictatorship, 60 members of the Roman Senate conspired to murder him in 44 B.C. One of the men was politician Marcus Brutus, a friend of Caesar's. With his dying breath, Caesar is thought to have uttered, *"Et tu, Brute?"* which means, "You too, Brutus?" Those words have become as famous as the man himself.

AUGUSTUS CAESAR
HE BROUGHT PEACE TO ROME

When Gaius Octavius was 18 years old, he learned that his great-uncle, Julius Caesar, had been murdered. In his will, Caesar named Octavius as his son. Caesar's old soldiers rallied around Octavius. The Senate liked him, too, and he ruled the empire along with Marc Antony and Lepidus.

Then, after some hard-fought wars, Lepidus was stripped of his power and Antony died, so that left Octavius in charge. He made himself emperor and was known from then on as Augustus, "the exalted one." He expanded the empire into Egypt, Spain, and Germany, but also achieved peace and prosperity at home for the next 200 years.

> Archaeologists excavated part of a Roman fort along Hadrian's Wall and found pieces of game boards that Roman guards would have used to pass the time.

HADRIAN
HE MADE BEARDS POPULAR

After Augustus died in A.D. 14, Rome didn't see an era of peace and prosperity for decades—not until emperor Hadrian took the throne in A.D. 117. For many reasons, he is one of Rome's most intriguing emperors.

- Hadrian loved to travel and learn new things. After his death, a Roman writer dubbed the emperor, "the explorer of everything interesting."
- He climbed Mount Etna, a 10,900-foot (3,322-m)-tall volcano in Sicily, just to see the sunrise.
- He made beard-wearing popular.
- He wrote poetry.
- He commissioned many beautiful buildings and temples, and his greatest monument is Hadrian's Wall. Built to protect Britain from invaders, this stone wall is 12 feet (3.7 m) high in places and 73 miles (117 km) long.

‹ EXPLORE ›
LIFE IN ANCIENT ROME

The four main chariot teams in ancient Rome were the Red, White, Blue, and Green Teams.

Romans would also sometimes sacrifice an animal to the gods before eating it, as shown in this art depiction of Roman life.

The ancient Romans had a pantheon of gods and goddesses that was similar to the Greek pantheon. Romans believed if they gave offerings to the gods, such as food, the gods would do them favors in return. Romans might visit a local temple once a day to do this. Every temple had priests who would accept the offerings.

At home, families might have an altar bearing three statues called lares. In the center would be a statue of a god or goddess, such as Vesta, goddess of the hearth. On either side of that statue would be a statue of a household spirit, usually depicted as a young person in a short tunic. Prayers and offerings were made to the lares, too.

TOGAS VS. TUNICS

A toga was a specific type of draped garment that, at certain times in history, could be worn only if you were a male citizen of Rome—someone with the right to vote and own property. A large piece of fabric, the toga was draped loosely over the body and was worn long, down to the ankles.

It's kind of difficult to get any real work done wearing a bulky toga, so most working people would wear a tunic instead, usually made of wool. These tunics were worn at knee length and made by sewing two pieces of fabric together, leaving holes for arms. Sometimes a belt was worn around the waist.

DANGEROUS GAMES

Two of the most popular forms of entertainment were chariot racing and gladiator fights.

Almost 200,000 people could gather in the Circus Maximus, a large stadium where the chariot races took place. Spectators rooted for their favorite team of racers as the chariots sped around the track. During these high-speed contests, there was a danger that the chariot could topple over or the rider could be thrown off. If that happened, the rider would most likely be trampled by horses.

Whereas chariot races could sometimes be deadly, gladiator competitions almost always ended in death. In these violent competitions, fighters were pitted against each other, and the only way to win was to kill your opponent. Most gladiators were criminals or slaves who were forced to fight.

Gladiators, like these reenactors, used weapons such as the short sword, curved dagger, and a three-pronged spear called a trident.

TREASURES OF ANCIENT ROME

It's beautiful inside the temple. Around the walls of the dome-shaped room are marble columns and life-size sculptures of gods and goddesses. The red light on your watch is blinking brightly now, and you follow the signal to one of the marble columns. A gleaming orange gem is embedded in the marble, and you carefully remove it.

"Got it," you whisper to Karma.

She nods across the temple. "Good," she says. "But I think we'd better get out of here."

Three Roman soldiers have spotted you, and they stomp toward you, yelling loudly.

> Some of the ancient aqueducts are still in use today.

THE AQUEDUCTS
A PRACTICAL TREASURE

Some experts say that the greatest treasure created by the ancient Romans wasn't a sculpture or a painting—it was the complex system of aqueducts that carried water throughout the city.

The Roman aqueducts were an engineering marvel. A total of 11 aqueduct systems brought water to the city from as far as 57 miles (92 km) away. In some places, the water flowed down stone arches. In most places, it traveled through underground pipes made of terra-cotta, stone, or other materials. The only thing powering the water through the aqueducts was the flow of gravity.

ROME
A.D. 130

This Roman statue is a herm of Dionysus. A herm was a statue usually used as a signpost or to mark a boundary.

Many Roman sculptures are copies of works from the classical Greek period.

ANCIENT TREASURES

THE PORTLAND VASE

The Portland Vase is one of the most famous artifacts handed down from ancient Rome. So what makes it so special?

IT TOOK SKILL. The vase is made of two layers of blown glass. After they cooled, the design was carved into the second, white layer of glass. That's very difficult to do without cracking the glass.

IT LASTED THROUGH THE AGES. This vase was probably made between A.D. 5 and 25. Experts think there was a pointed bottom part that broke off, but otherwise it's in beautiful condition.

IT'S MYSTERIOUS. The design shows several scenes of women and men. Cupid, the god who makes people fall in love, is in one scene. There is a snake in another scene. Experts can't agree on what kind of story the scenes are telling. Some think the vase might tell a love story and was given as a wedding gift.

You run as fast as you can with the Roman soldiers at your heels.

"If you can zap us to another time, you might want to do it now," says Karma.

You pull the idol from your backpack and press its head.

"Stick close!" you yell to Karma, and then the swirling light whisks you both away.

A.D. 1150

THE PORTAL LANDS YOU ON THE EDGE OF A STONE WALL.

YOU LOSE YOUR FOOTING,

AND KARMA GRABS YOU BEFORE YOU FALL.

"Thanks!" you say, steadying yourself. You look down to see that you and the explorer are on the edge of what looks like a giant, man-made pool. "My watch says it's A.D. 1150. But where are we?"

"I believe we might be in the Maya or Toltec era," replies Karma. "That there is what they call a cenote." She pronounces it say-NOH-tay.

"What's a cenote?" you ask.

"It's a sacred well," Karma explains.

You check the back of the idol's head and check out the new symbol that's appeared.

"It's the head of a jaguar," you say.

Karma turns and points to the towering city behind you. "Looks like we've landed in the ancient city of Chichén Itzá in Mexico."

North America

MEXICO

MEXICO

GULF OF MEXICO

MEXICO

BELIZE

GUATEMALA HONDURAS

PACIFIC OCEAN

EL SALVADOR

0   200   400 miles
0   200   400 kilometers

GULF OF MEXICO

MEXICO

Chichén Itzá

Yucatán Peninsula

Mexico City

CARIBBEAN SEA

PACIFIC OCEAN

- Maya Civilization 250 B.C.–A.D. 900
- Toltec Civilization A.D. 900–1100
- Area Containing Both Civilizations

EL CASTILLO PYRAMID

A path from the sacred cenote leads into the city, and takes you right to a huge pyramid with a flat top.

"Hey, I thought the only pyramids were in Egypt," you say.

"The Egyptians weren't the only ones to build them," Karma tells you. "After the Maya built this city, Toltec invaders came. They're the ones who built this pyramid we're looking at."

You gaze up at the steps leading to the top of the pyramid. "Can we climb it?" you ask, and Karma nods.

"Sure, why not?" she says. "But you'll have to keep up with my ninja-like skills."

EACH OF THE PYRAMID'S FOUR SIDES EXACTLY FACES IN ONE DIRECTION: NORTH, SOUTH, EAST, OR WEST.

SHADOW OF THE SERPENT

El Castillo may have another built-in secret. Every year, on the spring and autumn equinox, a shadow that looks like the body of a snake is created on the side of the pyramid that faces north. The shadow wriggles down the body of the pyramid and ends at the base of one of the sculpted serpent heads at the bottom of the steps.

CHICHÉN ITZA
A.D. 1150

The pyramid is 79 feet (24 m) high.

TEMPLE STATS

BUILT: About 10th century A.D.

LOCATION: The city of Chichén Itzá, on Mexico's Yucatán Peninsula

DEDICATED TO: A carving of a snake with feathers on the pyramid represents Quetzalcóatl—a god worshipped by the Maya (who called him Kukulcán) and the Toltec.

WHO MADE IT: Invaders of Chichén Itzá who were either Toltec, or who were influenced by Toltec culture

EACH SIDE OF THE PYRAMID HAS 91 STEPS. IF YOU COUNT THE STEP ON THE TOP PLATFORM, THAT'S 365 STEPS IN ALL—THE SAME AS THE NUMBER OF DAYS IN THE SOLAR CALENDAR.

A MYSTERIOUS ECHO

In 1998, an acoustic engineer named David Lubman was visiting El Castillo pyramid. He was curious about the sounds that bounced off the pyramid's steps. He clapped his hands at the bottom of the steps—and the sound of a bird chirping echoed back at him. And it isn't just any bird—it resembles the call of the quetzal, which was sacred to the Maya and associated with the god Quetzalcóatl. Lubman believes that the builders designed the pyramid to make the sound, but other experts think it could just be a coincidence.

⟨ EXPLORE ⟩
THE MAYA
AND TOLTEC

The Maya "Long Count" calendar plotted out 5,125 years, ending on December 21, 2012, which some people interpreted as the end of the world.

The city of Chichén Itzá was shaped by two different cultures: the Maya and the Toltec. The Maya founded the city somewhere around A.D. 600. Among other structures, they built a church and an observatory.

Around the tenth century A.D., invaders came to the city. They may have been Toltec, or just influenced by Toltec culture. They built the El Castillo pyramid and a large ball court.

When the Spanish invaded Mexico in the 16th century, they came to Chichén Itzá. The city was still sacred to the Maya but mostly deserted.

These columns appear on top of the Toltec temple of Tlahuizcalpantecuhtli, or "temple of the morning star," in Tula, Mexico. These detailed sculptures depict the god Quetzalcóatl in his guise as god of the dawn and Toltec warriors dressed for war.

RISE OF THE MAYA

The story of the Maya begins about 1500 B.C., when the native people of Mexico, Guatemala, and northern Belize began to settle in villages. They were farmers who grew corn, beans, and squash.

Then they began to build things out of stone, such as temples. Cities grew around these buildings, and by 250 B.C. the Classic period of Maya culture began. This period lasted until A.D. 900 and saw some of their great achievements: big cities; a system of hieroglyphic writing; advances in astronomy, including a sophisticated calendar; sculptures; and the construction of beautiful temples and pyramids.

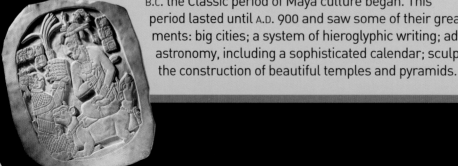

Centuries after the Toltec, the Aztec worshipped Quetzalcóatl as a god of writing and credited him with creating their calendar.

This stone warrior figure is a column once used to support a Toltec pyramid dedicated to Quetzalcóatl.

The god was sometimes portrayed as a snake with feathers, and sometimes as a man with a beard.

QUETZALCÓATL
GOD OF WAR

The Toltec achieved power in central Mexico from A.D. 900–1200. They worshipped the god Quetzalcóatl, whose name means "feathered serpent." He may have started out as a god of farming and water, but by the time the Toltec culture peaked, he was more of a war god.

The Toltec leader Topiltzin took the name of Quetzal-cóatl when he ruled during the tenth century A.D. The Toltec were known as warriors, but they were also great craftsmen who created statues, palaces, temples, and pyramids.

The dominance of the Toltec ended when the Chichimec people from the north attacked the Toltec capital city, Tula, around A.D. 1150.

95

ANIMALS OF THE YUCATÁN

When you get to the top of the Castillo pyramid, you look at the city below you in wonder. There are so many other temples and buildings to explore.

"Wish we could get inside here," Karma says. "The pyramid was built over an old temple, and inside that is a throne shaped like a jaguar."

You suddenly remember something. "Hey, the symbol on the idol looks like a jaguar."

Karma nods. "It's no wonder the Maya respected them. They're the largest big cat in South America, and they can be very dangerous."

KEEL-BILLED TOUCAN

These birds love to live in flocks, making their homes in hollow trees in tropical forests. They can be seen flying across the forest canopy in search of fruit to eat.

ANCIENT TREASURES

THE JAGUAR THRONE

Inside the Castillo pyramid, archaeologists found an older pyramid. They found this jaguar-shaped throne inside. The jaguar was sacred to the Maya, who worshipped a jaguar god. The statue is red and studded with precious green jade.

NORTHERN TAMANDUA

A member of the anteater family, a tamandua is smaller and lives in trees as well as on the ground. They use their tail to help them climb, and use their long, sticky tongue to grab ants out of their nests.

The jaguar's eyes are designed to help it see and hunt at night. During the day, it can't see as much detail and color.

The spots on a jaguar are called rosettes because they look like roses.

JAGUAR

TYPE: Mammal

HABITAT: Swamps, forests, deserts, scrublands

SIZE: Up to 9 feet (2.7 m) long, including tail, weighs up to 300 pounds (136 kg)

DIET: Capybara, peccary, birds, fish, and other small animals

LIFE SPAN: 12–15 years

WHY THEY'RE WORSHIPPED: To the Maya, the jaguar was a symbol of strength and power. Because the jaguar prowls at night, it was believed to rule the underworld.

The word "jaguar" comes from a Native American word meaning "he who kills with one leap."

EXPLORING THE CITY

>>> Walking back down the pyramid, you notice that the homing beacon is still blinking steadily—you're not sure if you're close to the gem or not.

"Let's explore some of the other buildings around here," you suggest.

As you search the city, you gaze at the Castillo pyramid once more.

That's when you notice a shadow snaking down one side of the pyramid. It looks like the body of a reptile, and merges with an enormous sculpture of a snake's head at the bottom of the stairs.

THE NUNNERY

This group of buildings, named by the Spanish because they reminded them of Spanish convents, are known as the Grupo de las Monjas. Built by the Maya before the Toltec invaders came, it shows off some of the most intricate sculpture and latticework. La Iglesia building, "the church" in Spanish, is one of the oldest at Chichén Itzá and features carvings of an armadillo, tortoise, crab, and snail. These animals, according to Maya legend, held up the sky.

MAYA GAMES

Could this have been ancient basketball? This ball court was used for playing a game called *tlachtli*, or *pok-ta-pok*. Wearing heavy padding to protect themselves, players tried to knock a heavy ball into the court of their opponent. After A.D. 900, two stone rings were placed on each side of the court, and the object became to get the ball through the rings. The ball likely represented the sun and the rings represented sunrise and sunset, or the spring and fall equinoxes.

TEMPLE OF THE WARRIORS

The Temple of the Warriors and the hundreds of columns that surround it were probably built around the tenth century A.D., when the invaders came. On top sits a type of statue called a Chac Mool, a man reclining with his stomach flat. Experts believe human sacrifices were carried out on these statues. They also think this building, with its large platforms on four sides, may have been the only structure in Chichén Itzá large enough for public gatherings.

The pok-ta-pok court was shaped like a capital letter I.

Pok-ta-pok was sometimes played as a ritual to reenact the ancient battle between good and evil. Some scholars believe that in those games, the leader of the losing team was sacrificed.

The afternoon sun shines on the shadow snake's head, and you see a shimmer catch the light. "The gem!" you cry, and you run to the pyramid and take a dark pink gem from the eye of the snake.

"Nice job," Karma says. "But you're on your own from here on in. I'm using my portal and getting out of here."

You say goodbye to Karma and activate the idol. A symbol of a sun appears in one of the two remaining circles. You're getting close now.

GUILLERMO DE ANDA
UNDERWATER ARCHAEOLOGIST

DIVING IN SACRED CAVES

It all started when he dove into a cave when he was just 15 years old.

"It was such a small cave, but I was fascinated," Guillermo de Anda remembers. "I thought, this is really what I want to do for the rest of my life."

So de Anda kept cave diving—searching for ancient artifacts. He traveled to Mexico's Yucatán Peninsula to explore the many cenotes, or sacred wells, there. Intrigued by the bones he discovered on these dives, he got a degree in bioarchaeology so he could study them. That led to a Ph.D. in Meso-American studies—and a lifelong fascination with the ancient people of Mexico.

The Sacred Cenote

De Anda has explored the cenotes in the city of Chichén Itzá and he believes four of them have special significance. If you were to draw a line connecting the four, they make a rectangle, with the Castillo pyramid in the center. De Anda says that to the Maya, the four cenotes represented the four sacred points of the universe, and they built the Castillo pyramid to represent the center of the universe.

The cenote north of the pyramid is known as the Sacred Cenote. De Anda has explored it many times. "It's only 50 feet [15 m] deep, but . . . the visibility is zero. There are lots of branches, and that makes it a little dangerous."

Despite the dangers, de Anda and his team use scuba gear and diving lights to discover amazing artifacts inside the cenote. There are human bones, some of which are the remains of human sacrifice; artifacts made of an alloy of copper and gold; and figures of animals and gods important to the Maya.

EXPLORER STATS

NAME: Guillermo de Anda

MISSION: To better understand in a more believable way what happened at the cenotes and to learn more about the people sacrificed there

HOME BASE: Mérida, Mexico

FUN FACT: He was the first Mexican to receive credentials to become a cave-diving instructor.

De Anda gets ready to descend into one of his research cenotes near Mérida, Mexico (left). When diving underwater, shafts of light make some cenotes look otherworldly (right).

De Anda has come to some important conclusions: "The Sacred Cenote was a very important place of pilgrimage to all of Central America." His evidence? Turquoise objects from the Chaco Canyon in New Mexico, which is about 2,500 miles (4,020 km) away.

"Every time we find answers, we find more questions," de Anda says—which means he won't stop diving anytime soon.

When the sun is directly overhead the Holtún cenote twice a year, it creates a vertical shaft of light that falls into the water. De Anda thinks that the Maya probably built a structure to catch the rays the same way.

STORIES OF THE BONES

De Anda can learn many things from the ancient peoples' bones he finds: their gender, what they ate, how they lived, how old they were when they died, and even where they were from. He can also learn why they died, and the reasons are sometimes surprising.

"Caves and cenotes represent life and death, dark and light, up and down," de Anda explains. He says the Maya were drawn to these places, and priests used them to perform rituals.

"In times of trouble or drought they would go to the cenotes to ask for rain," de Anda says. Sometimes priests even offered human sacrifices to appease the gods. But not all the bones he finds were the result of sacrifices. Sometimes, the bones of ancestors might have been buried in the cenote—either as an offering, or to make up for something bad the ancestor might have done, "to balance the good and the bad."

WHEN **THE BRIGHT, SWIRLING** LIGHT OF THE PORTAL DISAPPEARS, YOU SEE A PEACEFUL FIELD FULL OF ROWS OF TALL CORNSTALKS.

>>> Women in long dresses and shawls are working in the field. It's chillier than it was in Chichén Itzá, and you shiver.

"Nothing like mountain air, is there?" a voice behind you asks.

Startled, you turn around—and see a young woman standing behind you. She has a hip, jagged haircut, and her green eyes have a friendly look. She's dressed in cargo shorts with an olive green vest. Immediately, you can tell she's a photographer because she's equipped herself with two cameras strapped to her back and a smartphone.

"Whoa, I've gotta get pics of this place! Oh, I'm Maria Selva," she says with a strong Brazilian accent. "Guy heard that Karma bailed on you, so here I am."

"Thanks," you say. "I've only got two more gems left to find. But I don't see a temple here."

Maria smiles. "Look up!"

You follow her gaze upward—and see a tall mountain peak just behind you. It looks like there's a city on top.

PERU

PERU South America

Inca Empire
A.D. 1520

ECUADOR

PERU

BOLIVIA

PACIFIC
OCEAN

CHILE

ARGENTINA

PERU

Lima

Machu
Picchu

Cusco

PACIFIC
OCEAN

0   100   200 miles
0   100   200 kilometers

THE ANDES MOUNTAINS

The air feels colder and crisper as you and Maria make your way up your side of the mountain. Snow-capped peaks kiss the sky in the distance, but green grass is growing on the mountain. It's a tasty meal for the herds of pale brown llamas grazing nearby.

"So what is the name of this place?" you ask Maria, nodding toward the city on the mountaintop.

"Machu Picchu," she replies. "It was built by the Inca people here in the Andes in Peru."

CHINCHILLA

These rodents were almost hunted to extinction by humans, who wanted their thick, soft fur. In the Andes, they hide among the crevices in the rocks during the day and come out at night to search for plants to eat. Chinchillas have also become popular pets in many parts of the world.

CALLING THE ANDES HOME

The Andes are a system, or range, of mountains that run along the west coast of South America. This line of plateaus and peaks stretches for 5,500 miles (8,850 km). Some of the Andes mountains are among the highest in the world.

The mountain range is the longest in the world and passes through seven countries—Venezuela, Colombia, Peru, Ecuador, Bolivia, Chile, and Argentina. In Peru, where Machu Picchu is located, the land around the Andes mountains is made up of high, flat plains or plateaus. The weather at these high elevations can be cold—below 50°Fahrenheit (10°C) during the day, and below freezing at night.

The city of Machu Picchu is 7,972 feet (2,430 m) above sea level.

ANDEAN CONDOR

The Andean condor is one of the largest flying birds in the world. The ancient Inca believed the condor delivered the sun to the sky each morning.

A hooked beak helps the condor tear the flesh off the carcasses of wild and domestic animals. The bird's wingspan can reach over ten feet (3 m). There are no feathers on the head of this bird.

Like a cow, a llama will eat grass, regurgitate it, and chew on it as cud.

A llama can carry as much as 75 pounds (34 kg) up to 20 miles (32 km).

LLAMA

TYPE: Mammal

HABITAT: Mountains

SIZE: About 4 feet (1.2 m) up to the shoulder, weighs up to 250 pounds (113 kg)

DIET: Grass

ANCIENT USES: Carried goods over rough mountain terrain; wool used to make blankets and clothing; hide used to make leather goods; waste burned for fuel; meat for food

THE CITY OF THE INCA

Machu Picchu was probably built around A.D. 1450 and people lived there until about 1550. The structures, including steps, walls, buildings, homes, and temples, all appear to have been built in the mountainside.

Experts believe that the emperor who might be responsible for building Machu Picchu is Pachacuti Inca Yupanqui, who reigned from A.D. 1438 to 1471. Under his rule, the Inca quickly expanded their empire from central Peru into southern Peru and up north into Ecuador. The capital city of his empire was Cusco, but Machu Picchu might have been a kind of royal retreat—a vacation home for kings.

many of the structures in Machu Picchu
er so expertly that the blade of a knife
een them. Some wonder how the Inca
without the use of modern tools.

Experts believe that the Spanish conquerors never found Machu Picchu.

THE SPANISH CONQUEST

The Inca Empire fell at the hands of Francisco Pizarro, a conqueror from Spain. He had heard stories of the Inca's wealth and wanted it for Spain. Although Pizarro had only a small army, the Inca Empire was weakened by a civil war and Pizarro won many battles. In A.D. 1532, he kidnapped the Inca emperor Atahualpa, who offered Pizarro a room full of gold and silver in exchange for his freedom. Pizarro took the treasure—and had Atahualpa executed anyway. It was a tragic end to a great empire.

WHO WERE THE INCA?

WHERE THEY LIVED: South America, from Ecuador down to Chile, and from the coast of the Pacific Ocean to the Andes

POPULATION: Up to 12 million

LANGUAGE: Quechua, which is still spoken in the Andes today. The ancient Inca did not have a form of writing.

GOVERNMENT: The Inca were ruled by an emperor who was thought to be descended from the sun god.

ACHIEVEMENTS: The Inca were great farmers. They were the first people who figured out how to grow potatoes. Their craftspeople were expert weavers, and they made objects of gold and other metals. They made musical instruments such as flutes, bells, and trumpets. And they built complex structures, walkways, and bridges in the difficult terrain of the Andes.

Within 100 years after it was built, the Inca had deserted their city in the clouds. Why? Nobody knows for sure. One theory is that it was too difficult to get water up the mountain for people to live there. Archaeologists are still looking for the answer.

Throughout Machu Picchu, thousands of steps were carved into the rock under the soil. They connected the places where residents lived, farmed, and worshipped.

TEMPLE OF THE SUN

>>> The homing beacon on your watch leads you and Maria to one of the stone temples. You can see the lime green gem gleaming on the temple door, but a man is guarding the temple.

"How are we going to get it?" you whisper to Maria.

"Leave that to me," she says.

She slips off, and a few seconds later you hear a big commotion. You turn to see a small herd of llamas racing across the terraces, chased by some screaming farmers. The man guarding the temple joins the chase.

"Nice job," you say, as you and Maria quickly run to the temple door.

TEMPLE STATS

BUILT: Around A.D. 1450

LOCATION: The Urubamba Valley in Peru

OTHER NAMES: Torreón

WHO MADE IT: Some researchers believe that the temple, and the city of Machu Picchu, were built under the rule of the Inca emperor Pachacuti.

WHAT IT WAS USED FOR: There are multiple theories, but one is that it was an observatory. The Sun Temple's windows may have been deliberately placed by the Inca to watch certain constellations on the winter and summer solstices.

THE SUN TEMPLE

Nobody knows what the Inca actually called this sprawling structure, but researchers think it was a religious center built to honor the sun. It's the highest point in the city, so it has the best view of the sky above. On the winter solstice, sunlight streams directly through one of the windows. The Pleiades constellation, which was important to many Andean cultures, can also be seen through this window.

108

Inside the temple was an altar stone where Inca priests would offer sacrifices to the gods.

ANCIENT TREASURES

THE LOST INCA GOLD

Stories of a lost horde of Inca gold are legendary. Some say that explorer Francisco Pizarro received only part of the gold ransom for emperor Atahualpa. The rest—a huge store of gold—is said to be buried in a secret cave in Peru.

Many have searched for the gold, but none have ever found it. Many think the gold was taken long ago. Others think it's still out there somewhere, but lost forever due to earthquakes that regularly hit the heavily forested mountains.

This gold mask is just one example of the many gold treasures produced by the Inca.

FIND THIS GOLDEN LLAMA IN THE TEMPLE RUN GAME!

The Inca believed that the closer the temple was to the sky, the more effective their rituals would be.

The final symbol appears on the idol after you get the gem in place: a drawing of what looks like a warrior's face with his mouth open in a scary snarl.

"Looks Aztec to me," Maria says. "Cool!"

You press the idol's head. "We'd better hurry before that guard gets back!"

YOU LEAVE MACHU PICCHU BEHIND AND

TOUCH DOWN IN FRONT OF ANOTHER PYRAMID.

This one has a tiny building on top. "So the Aztec had pyramids too?" you ask. Maria nods. "Yup. This one is located in what we now know as Santa Cecilia, Mexico. That little building up there is a temple."

"Cool," you say. "You think the gem is in there?"

"What does your watch say?" Maria asks.

Your watch isn't blinking. "No gem. But it does say that we're in A.D. 1510."

Maria looks thoughtful. "I think we need to take a little hike. We're not far from where the capital of the Aztec Empire was in 1510—the city of Tenochtitlan."

"I've never heard of any ruins there," you say.

"That's because the city was destroyed and Mexico City was built on top of it," Maria explains. "So we're pretty lucky. We're about to explore a city that nobody has seen for hundreds of years!"

She hands you a canteen of water. "Have a sip. It's going to be a long walk."

North America

MEXICO

0   200   400 miles
0   200   400 kilometers

MEXICO

GULF OF
MEXICO

Mexico City• —Tenochtitlan

CARIBBEAN
SEA

GULF OF
MEXICO

MEXICO

GUATEMALA

PACIFIC OCEAN

PACIFIC OCEAN

☐ Aztec Civilization A.D. 1400–1521

THE MIGHTY AZTEC

"You know," Maria says, as you approach the city, "if we had arrived a few years later, the Spanish would be attacking. We've arrived at a good time."

"I'm just glad we've arrived," you say, taking another swig from the canteen. You've been hiking for hours, and you're exhausted.

"We need to be careful when we enter the city," Maria warns. "The Aztec were fierce warriors. I'm not sure how they felt about strangers."

The Aztec people first arrived in central Mexico around A.D. 1200.

FROM FARMERS TO WARRIORS

The Aztec Empire flourished in Mexico during the 15th and early 16th centuries A.D. But before they became conquerors, the Aztec people were prosperous thanks to their advances in agriculture. They developed complex irrigation systems, and figured out how to turn swampland into farmland.

Aztec emperors began to conquer other lands, and the empire reached as far as what is now Nicaragua and Honduras. The Aztec demanded tribute from the people they ruled—gifts in the form of riches, food, and even people for human sacrifices. They believed that their sun god, Tonatiuh, required offerings of human hearts.

The Aztec ruled their empire for 200 years—until Spanish explorers came and ended it all.

THE FALL OF MONTEZUMA II

Montezuma II took the Aztec throne in A.D. 1502. The empire had already expanded to parts of Central America, and resentment against the Aztec was building. The conquered tribes hated their new rulers. But things were about to change.

In 1519, the explorer Hernán Cortés arrived. With his white skin and beard, he resembled the images of the god of the Aztec, Quetzalcóatl. So the Aztec feared Cortés, and tribes conquered by the Aztec helped him because they wanted to see their conquerors overthrown.

But Montezuma II wanted to get rid of Cortés, so in 1520 he welcomed him to Tenochtitlan in hopes of capturing him. What happened next we only know from the records of the Spanish invaders. But Cortés captured Montezuma II instead! According to accounts, when Montezuma II was allowed to appear in public, his own people, angry at his weakness, hurled stones and arrows at him. He suffered wounds and died from them three days later. A year after, the Aztec Empire fell to Spain.

The Aztec developed a calendar based on the Maya calendar, with 365 days.

Cortés needed the help of other allies to conquer the Aztec. When he left for Mexico, he had only 508 soldiers and 100 sailors with him.

113

‹ EXPLORE ›
THE PYRAMID OF CHOLULA

Today, visitors to Cholula can see the Spanish church, which sits atop the old pyramid with the impressive Popocatépetl volcano behind it.

Located about six miles (10 km) southwest of Tenochtitlan, Cholula was the second biggest city in Mexico during the time of the Aztec. Dedicated to Quetzalcóatl, the city may have had as many as 100,000 residents and as many as 365 temples. The residents were craftspeople who made fabrics and pottery and traded them.

The Cholula and the Aztec had an alliance, and like the Aztec, the people of Cholula met a tragic end at the hand of Hernán Cortés. Before marching his troops into Tenochtitlan, Cortés stopped in Cholula and massacred an estimated 3,000 people there.

The Spanish took over the city and built churches on top of the old temples, including the Great Pyramid of Tepanapa, known today as the Great Pyramid of Cholula. The churches still stand today, making Cholula a popular city for tourists.

ANCIENT TREASURES

THE CHOLULA FIGURINES

Archaeologists began to excavate Cholula in the 1930s. Since then, small, clay figurines have been discovered at Cholula. Most of them appear human—either heads, full bodies, or other body parts. There are male and female figurines, and many are believed to be of Tlaloc, the rain god.

As god of rain, Tlaloc had a light and a dark side. Rain, of course, is needed for crops to grow, but drought and floods can be deadly. He was sometimes shown carrying rattles, which he could use to make thunder.

When Cortés came to Cholula, trees had grown over it, and the Spanish thought it was just a big hill. They built a church on top of it.

If you visit the pyramid today, you can tour the tunnels underneath the pyramid's base.

THE GREAT PYRAMID

One of the temples in Cholula was a pyramid that is one of the largest in the world. The Great Pyramid was only about 177 feet (54 m) high—not even half the height of Egypt's Great Pyramid—but it has a wide base that covers nearly 45 acres (18 ha). That gives the pyramid enormous space inside.

The pyramid may have been a site for pilgrimages. Seashells were found at an altar to Quetzalcóatl, probably brought as offerings by people who lived on the coast.

The pyramid was also used for human sacrifice. The bodies of children have been found by an altar, and it is believed that they were sacrificed to Tlaloc, the god of rain.

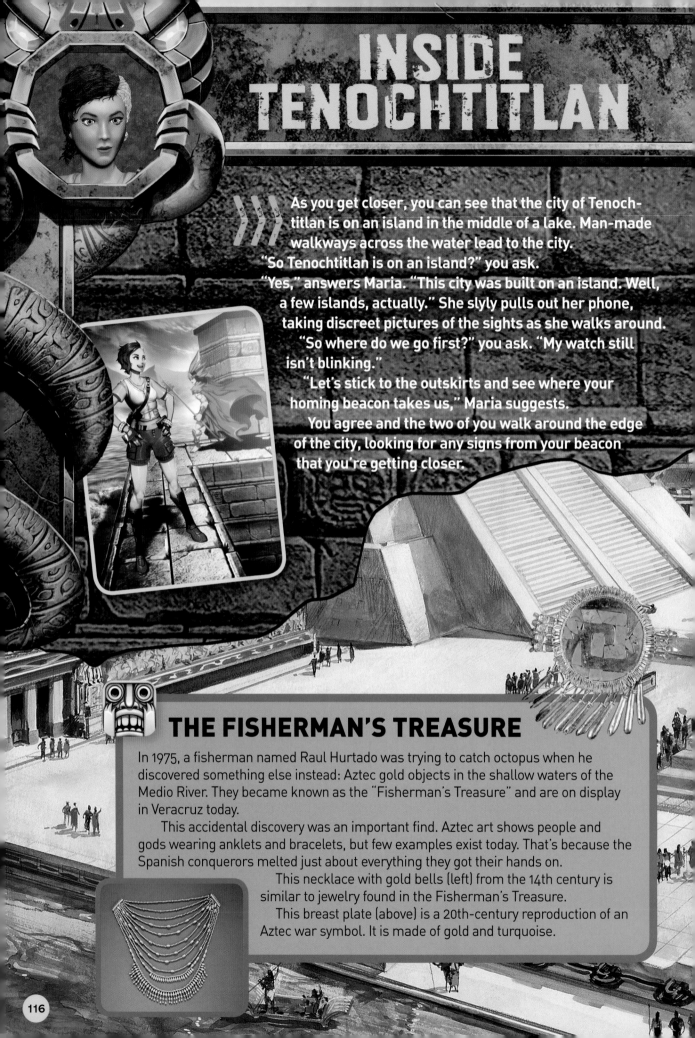

INSIDE TENOCHTITLAN

>>> As you get closer, you can see that the city of Tenoch-titlan is on an island in the middle of a lake. Man-made walkways across the water lead to the city.

"So Tenochtitlan is on an island?" you ask.

"Yes," answers Maria. "This city was built on an island. Well, a few islands, actually." She slyly pulls out her phone, taking discreet pictures of the sights as she walks around.

"So where do we go first?" you ask. "My watch still isn't blinking."

"Let's stick to the outskirts and see where your homing beacon takes us," Maria suggests.

You agree and the two of you walk around the edge of the city, looking for any signs from your beacon that you're getting closer.

THE FISHERMAN'S TREASURE

In 1975, a fisherman named Raul Hurtado was trying to catch octopus when he discovered something else instead: Aztec gold objects in the shallow waters of the Medio River. They became known as the "Fisherman's Treasure" and are on display in Veracruz today.

This accidental discovery was an important find. Aztec art shows people and gods wearing anklets and bracelets, but few examples exist today. That's because the Spanish conquerors melted just about everything they got their hands on.

This necklace with gold bells (left) from the 14th century is similar to jewelry found in the Fisherman's Treasure.

This breast plate (above) is a 20th-century reproduction of an Aztec war symbol. It is made of gold and turquoise.

TENOCHTITLAN
A.D. 1510

Getting around the city was easy because it was laid out in a grid pattern. The city builders were inspired by the grid pattern used to lay out the ancient Mexican city of Teotihuacán, which had been built 1,000 years earlier.

BURIED IN TIME

Many of the great buildings of Tenochtitlan were destroyed during battles with the Spanish. When they took over the city, they razed what was left and built the capital of New Spain on top of the ruins. The Spanish named the city Mexico City, which today is the capital city of Mexico, with almost nine million residents.

Finding traces of the great Aztec Empire in the streets of Mexico City isn't easy, but pieces of one great temple still stand. Visitors can explore the ruins of the Templo Mayor in the heart of the city. Electric company workers discovered the ruins in 1978 when they unearthed a carved stone disc with a carving of an Aztec moon goddess. Further excavation revealed additional parts of the temple and artifacts. They are all on display at the Templo Mayor Museum.

CITY ON A LAKE

The builders of Tenochtitlan placed the city on two small islands in the middle of Lake Texcoco. As the city grew, they expanded it by creating artificial islands where they grew produce. Then they connected everything to the mainland with three causeways, or raised roadways. People traveled through the city on streets and canals. When finished, it took up five square miles (13 sq km) and was inhabited by about 400,000 residents at its height in 1519.

THE SACRED PRECINCT

The homing beacon leads you inside Tenochtitlan. There are bright colors all around you, from the clothing the Aztec are wearing to the blue-and-red painted pyramids rising in the city center.

You and Maria manage to blend into the crowds until you reach a walled complex in the middle of the city. Carved serpents decorate the wall.

"I think the gem is somewhere inside," you say, looking at the blinking beacon.

"This is the Sacred Precinct and inside is the Templo Mayor," Maria explains. "It's the heart of the empire." Your homing beacon is going crazy, and you know the gem must be in the temple.

The walls of the Sacred Precinct were decorated with images of serpents.

THE SACRED PRECINCT

The wealthiest Aztec lived just outside the walls of the city's sacred center. In those neighborhoods, you would find palaces, gardens, and zoos. Inside the walls was a square of about 1,140 by 990 feet (347 by 302 m) that could hold up to 8,000 people.

Priests of the Aztec gods lived here, and there were schools for boys training to be priests. But the biggest feature of the Sacred Precinct was the colorfully painted temples to the gods, including the Templo Mayor.

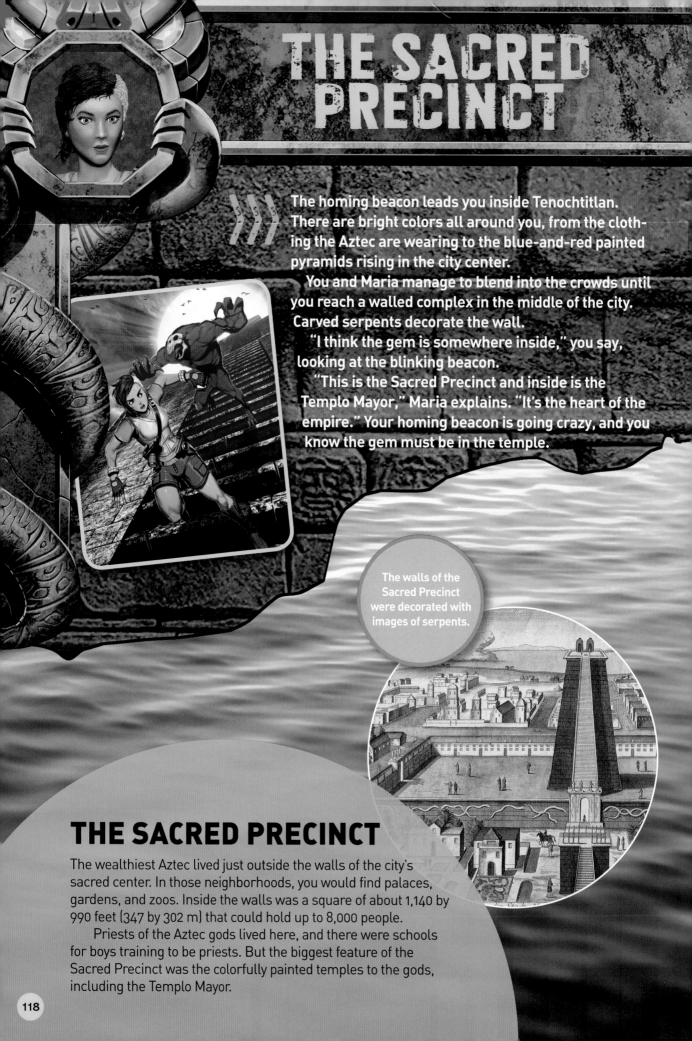

TENOCHTITLAN
A.D. 1510

TEMPLE STATS

BUILT: Building took place beginning in 1325, when the city was founded, and continued through the next century

LOCATION: What is today known as Mexico City

DEDICATED TO: Two Aztec gods: the sun and war god Huitzilopochtli and the rain god Tlaloc

WHO MADE IT: Each time a new Aztec emperor was crowned, he likely ordered changes and improvements to the temple.

The Templo Mayor is made up of two pyramids side by side, with a temple on top of each one. It stands about 90 feet (27 m) high.

Pushing your way to the front of the crowd, you see a small sky-blue gem gleaming in the base of the Templo Mayor.

You place the final gem in the idol, and it begins to glow brightly. The Aztec priests see it and start to point and shout. You and Maria look at each other helplessly. There's only one place to run. Up!

You and Maria climb the steps to the top of the Templo Mayor. "Hurry!" Maria urges. "These guys are big fans of human sacrifice!"

Trembling, you take out the idol and activate it. The idol's light explodes, sending you and Maria hurtling through time and space.

"That was fast!"

When the light fades you see Guy Dangerous standing there.

"What do you mean, fast?" you ask, looking around. "And where's Maria? She transported with me."

Guy shrugs. "She always lands on two feet. So, do you have all the gems?"

You hold out the idol.

"Great!" Guy says. "We just need to put it in place, and . . ."

"Aaaaaiiiiiieeeeeeeeeee!"

"Run!" you yell.

You and Guy charge out of the cave before the demon monkeys can trap you inside. You tear along the crumbling walkways of Angkor, following Guy. He knows the city like the back of his hand, making quick turns and jumping over obstacles to avoid the monkeys. It's not easy to keep up. Then Guy turns into a small stone temple, one you haven't seen before. Vines brush against your face as you follow him inside the entrance.

On the back wall of the temple is a stone altar with a small pedestal on top.

"The idol goes there," Guy says, pointing.

Your hands are trembling as you climb up the altar. Looking behind you, you see the demon monkeys and their glowing eyes bursting through the entrance.

"Hurry!" Guy yells.

You place the idol on top of the pedestal, and a brilliant light explodes, filling the temple. As the light beams hit the demon monkeys, they disappear, one by one vanishing in a bright flash of light.

When the light fades, there is nothing left in the temple except for you, Guy, and an eerie green smoke that swirls around you. Finally even the smoke disappears.

"Are they gone?" you ask.

"For now," Guy says. "But you never know with demon monkeys. They have a habit of popping up when you least expect them to."

You nod. "Well, I'll be happy if I don't see them for a while."

Guy grins at you. "So, you just saved the world. What do you want to do now?"

"I wouldn't mind seeing more temples."

"Sure thing," Guy says, and then he takes off at a sprint.

"Wait for me!" you cry as you run after him. Something tells you that as long as you're with Guy, you're going to be running a lot!

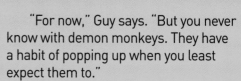

EXPLORE MORE

WEBSITES

Ancient Greeks: Athens
Explore ancient Greece with photos, fun facts, activities, and more.
bbc.co.uk/schools/primaryhistory/ancient_greeks/athens

Angkor Temples: The Ultimate Guide to Angkor Wat & the Angkor Ruins
Find photos and information on ten temples in the Angkor complex.
angkortemples.org

Animals
Search for facts and photos of animals from all over the world.
animals.nationalgeographic.com/animals

Archaeology
National Geographic brings you the latest in discoveries of the ancient world.
science.nationalgeographic.com/science/archaeology

Countries
Learn more about all of the countries in this book.
kids.nationalgeographic.com/kids/places

Dress the Roman Soldier
What kind of gear did a Roman soldier wear? Find out on this interactive page from the Birmingham Museums and Art Gallery.
schoolsliaison.org.uk/kids/romancent.htm

Petra, Jordan
Learn more about Petra from the American Museum of Natural History.
amnh.org/exhibitions/past-exhibitions/petra

Stonehenge, England
Videos, photos, and facts about the history and mysteries of the monument.
history.com/topics/stonehenge

VIDEOS

**Mummy Science:
The Inside Story**
Scientists at the Smithsonian National Museum of Natural History use imaging technology to get a closer look at mummies.
mnh.si.edu/exhibits/eternal-life/mummy-science.cfm

**Mysteries of the
Lost Temples videos**
Discover the mysteries behind the amazing ancient civilizations that built Angkor Wat, Chichén Itzá, Machu Picchu, and other sites in these short videos from National Geographic.
nationalgeographic.com/history/ancient/lost-tombs/angkor-wat-video.html

**People & Places:
Tombs of Ancient Egypt**
Take a video tour of Egypt's tombs.
video.nationalgeographic.com/video/kids/people-places-kids/egypt-tombs-kids

BOOKS FROM NATIONAL GEOGRAPHIC

The Golden King: The World of Tutankhamun
Zahi Hawass
2006

Hidden Treasures of Ancient Egypt
Zahi Hawass
2004

How to Be series
Learn how people of the ancient worlds lived.

How to Be an Ancient Greek Athlete
How to Be an Aztec Warrior
How to Be an Egyptian Princess
How to Be a Roman Soldier
How to Be a Samurai Warrior

If Stones Could Speak: Unlocking the Secrets of Stonehenge
Marc Aronson and Mike Parker Pearson
2010

Investigates: Ancient Civilizations series
Brings archaeology to life with a number of ancient civilizations featured in this book, including:

Ancient Aztec
Ancient China
Ancient Egypt
Ancient Greece

Ancient Inca
Ancient Maya
Ancient Rome

Mummies of the Pharaohs
Melvin and Gilda Berger
2001

National Geographic Kids Everything Ancient Egypt
Crispin Boyer With Egyptologist James P. Allen
2012

National Geographic Treasuries
Author Donna Jo Napoli and artist Christina Balit bring readers traditional myths from the ancient world.

Treasury of Egyptian Mythology
Treasury of Greek Mythology

Tutankhamun: The Golden King and the Great Pharaohs
Betsy M. Bryan, Suzanne Mubarak, and Zahi Hawass
2008

Voices of Ancient Egypt
Kay Winters, Illustrated by Barry Moser
2003

MUSEUMS

The British Museum
London, England
This museum exhibits artifacts from ancient civilizations all over the world, including the Aztec, Egyptians, and Greeks.

The Grand Egyptian Museum
Giza, Egypt
Scheduled to open in 2015, this museum will contain the largest collection of ancient Egyptian artifacts in the world.

Museo Nacional de Antropología (National Museum of Anthropology)
Mexico City, Mexico
Contains treasures and artifacts from the Maya and Aztec.

Smithsonian National Museum of Natural History
Washington, D.C., U.S.A.
Check out their "Eternal Life in Ancient Egypt" exhibit.

INDEX

PHOTO CREDITS

CREDITS

Published by the National Geographic Society
Gary E. Knell, *President and Chief Executive Officer*
John M. Fahey, *Chairman of the Board*
Declan Moore, *Executive Vice President; President, Publishing and Travel*
Melina Gerosa Bellows, *Publisher and Chief Creative Officer, Books, Kids, and Family*

Prepared by the Book Division
Hector Sierra, *Senior Vice President and General Manager*
Nancy Laties Feresten, *Senior Vice President, Kids Publishing and Media*
Jennifer Emmett, *Vice President, Editorial Director, Kids Books*
Eva Absher-Schantz, *Design Director, Kids Publishing and Media*
Jay Sumner, *Director of Photography, Kids Publishing*
R. Gary Colbert, *Production Director*
Jennifer A. Thornton, *Director of Managing Editorial*

Staff for This Book
Kate Olesin, *Editor*
Amanda Larsen, *Art Director and Designer*
Hillary Leo, *Photo Editor*
Paige Towler, *Editorial Assistant*
Jennifer Agresta, *Researcher*
Allie Allen, Sanjida Rashid, *Design Production Assistants*
Margaret Leist, *Photo Assistant*
Carl Mehler, *Director of Maps*
Michael McNey and Martin S. Walz, *Map Research and Production*
Grace Hill, *Associate Managing Editor*
Joan Gossett, *Production Editor*
Lewis R. Bassford, *Production Manager*
Susan Borke, *Legal and Business Affairs*

Production Services
Phillip L. Schlosser, *Senior Vice President*
Chris Brown, *Vice President, NG Book Manufacturing*
George Bounelis, *Senior Production Manager*
Nicole Elliott, *Director of Production*
Rachel Faulise, *Manager*
Robert L. Barr, *Manager*

For Imangi Studios, LLC
Walter Devins
Jason Flack
Natalia Luckyanova
Jeff Shepherd
Keith Shepherd
Jeremiah Washburn

The National Geographic Society is one of the world's largest nonprofit scientific and educational organizations. Founded in 1888 to "increase and diffuse geographic knowledge," the Society's mission is to inspire people to care about the planet. It reaches more than 400 million people worldwide each month through its official journal, *National Geographic*, and other magazines; National Geographic Channel; television documentaries; music; radio; films; books; DVDs; maps; exhibitions; live events; school publishing programs; interactive media; and merchandise. National Geographic has funded more than 10,000 scientific research, conservation, and exploration projects and supports an education program promoting geographic literacy.

For more information, please visit nationalgeographic .com, call 1-800-NGS LINE (647-5463), or write to the following address:
National Geographic Society
1145 17th Street N.W.
Washington, D.C. 20036-4688 U.S.A.

Visit us online at nationalgeographic.com/books

For librarians and teachers: ngchildrensbooks.org

More for kids from National Geographic:
kids.nationalgeographic.com

For information about special discounts for bulk purchases, please contact National Geographic Books Special Sales: ngspecsales@ngs.org

For rights or permissions inquiries, please contact National Geographic Books Subsidiary Rights: ngbookrights@ngs.org

Hardcover ISBN: 978-1-4263-1780-4
Reinforced Library Binding ISBN: 978-1-4263-1781-1

Printed in the United States of America
14/WOR/1

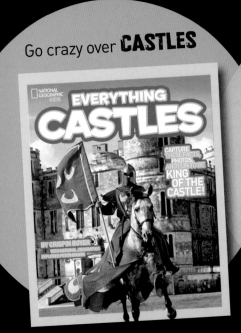

A BUSY TEMPLE

Archaeologists can get a picture of what Ta Prohm was like in the 12th century thanks to an inscription on the temple written in Sanskrit. It gives many details about the people and daily life there:

- 12,640 residents
- 2,740 officials
- 2,232 assistants
- 615 dancers
- 512 silk beds
- 260 statues of gods
- 35 diamonds
- 18 high priests

The trees growing over Ta Prohm are fig, banyan, and kapok trees.

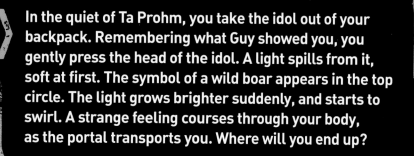

In the quiet of Ta Prohm, you take the idol out of your backpack. Remembering what Guy showed you, you gently press the head of the idol. A light spills from it, soft at first. The symbol of a wild boar appears in the top circle. The light grows brighter suddenly, and starts to swirl. A strange feeling courses through your body, as the portal transports you. Where will you end up?

< MEET AN EXPLORER >

ROLAND FLETCHER
ARCHAEOLOGIST

UNCOVERING ANGKOR'S MYSTERIES

EXPLORER STATS

NAME: Roland Fletcher

MISSION: To reassess the urban extent, settlement pattern, economy, and demise of Angkor in Cambodia.

HOME BASE: University of Sydney, Australia

CURRENT PROJECT: Greater Angkor Project

TEAM: Damian Evans; Christophe Pottier; Miriam Stark; Chhay Rachna; the APSARA Authority; and EFEO (French School of Asian Studies), which has worked in Angkor for about a century.

In the middle of Angkor is a walled and moated enclosure, about 3.5 square miles (9 sq km), called Angkor Thom. Some scholars think Angkor Thom was a self-contained city. But archaeologist Roland Fletcher and his team have other ideas.

Fletcher thinks of all of Angkor as a big sprawling city, like Los Angeles. "Our argument would be that Angkor Thom is like downtown. It is in the middle of central Angkor. Then all around, stretching far across the landscape, were suburbs. Between the 12th and 13th century A.D. Angkor covered almost 1,000 square kilometers [386 sq mi]," he says.

The difficulty in testing this theory is that between the 17th and 20th centuries, a dense jungle grew and buried Angkor. Today it still covers central Angkor. Finding out what lies beneath that jungle is a challenge—but Fletcher and his team have found a way.

Mapping the Jungle

The project began with the work of French scholar Christophe Pottier, who surveyed the southern half of Angkor in the 1990s. He used "his legs, a motorbike, aerial photography, and his eyeballs," remembers Fletcher.

Then Fletcher and his colleague Damian Evans, a remote-sensing specialist, joined the effort, contributing even more information to the growing map of the whole of Angkor. They used airborne radar, which collects data from a plane. The airborne radar showed a very spread-out, low-density city with canals, roads, mounds where houses would have been, and thousands of water tanks.

In 2012, the team focused their efforts on mapping central Angkor hidden under the forest. They made a breakthrough using a laser mapping method called

A helicopter with LiDAR attached (left) flies over Angkor in 2012. LiDAR captures images like these (right) which help scientists studying the region.

LiDAR (Light Detection and Ranging). It revealed even more details showing a grid pattern of streets throughout central Angkor, both inside Angkor Thom and far beyond its walls, connected with the suburbs. Though scientists already knew of the road grid in Angkor Thom, the fact that it existed beyond Angkor Thom was astonishing.

"The other magical piece of information is the new way that we understand Angkor Wat," Fletcher says. "There is an enclosure around the temple, and the LiDAR shows for sure that there were people living there—and even more outside the enclosure."

HOW LIDAR WORKS

How does LiDAR know what's under all those vines and trees? It starts in the air, on a helicopter or some other aerial platform.

From there, a laser light beam is aimed at a target on the ground. When the light hits an object, it bounces back and the LiDAR equipment picks up the return signal. It combines these findings with a lot of other data (including GPS data) to create a three-dimensional picture of the target below.

LiDAR can target something on the ground as small as "about six inches [15 cm] horizontally and vertically," says Fletcher. "You could see, in principle, a thing the size of a laptop computer."

Fletcher discusses excavation work with his APSARA colleagues.

9000 B.C.

THE LIGHT FINALLY FADES, AND YOU BLINK.

YOU'RE NOT IN TA PROHM TEMPLE ANYMORE.

It's eerily quiet. As you look around, you see that you're on top of a hill. Tall pillars shaped like the letter *T* rise up around you.

"This must be Göbekli Tepe," you say, and your voice echoes off the stones.

All of a sudden, you hear a loud groan. You turn to see Guy rubbing the back of his head, "Not the most graceful landing, but, hey, we made it!"

The face of the watch on your wrist lights up. You almost forgot that Guy gave it to you. A date is flashing: 9000 B.C. A chill goes through you as you realize—you're a long, long way from home.